ASK
SUZE

. . . ABOUT LOVE AND MONEY

ALSO BY SUZE ORMAN

You've Earned It, Don't Lose It
The 9 Steps to Financial Freedom
The Courage to Be Rich

Riverhead Books
a member of
Penguin Putnam Inc.
New York
2000

ASK
SUZE

◆

...ABOUT LOVE
AND MONEY

SUZE ORMAN

RIVERHEAD BOOKS
a member of
Penguin Putnam Inc.
375 Hudson Street
New York, NY 10014

ISBN 1-57322-421-9
GEN-833

Printed in the United States of America
1   3   5   7   9   10   8   6   4   2

This book is printed on acid-free paper. ∞

Book design by Deborah Kerner and Claire Vaccaro

ACKNOWLEDGMENTS

I'd like to thank Frederick Hertz, an attorney in Oakland, California, who works with straight and gay couples, for his invaluable expertise and insights, and Peter J. Smith for his help in compiling this book.

ASK
SUZE

. . . ABOUT LOVE AND MONEY

INTRODUCTION

Falling in love is simple—right? But sooner or later, in any relationship, disagreements crop up, and love becomes a complicated venture indeed. Can you guess what one of the most common subjects of disagreement between couples, married or unmarried, is? No surprises here—it's money. I hear it all the time: "Money is ruining our relationship," or "We were doing just fine until we started talking about our finances." Arguments over money trigger separation and divorce in more cases than you can imagine. And this is because the emotions people feel for their money, people's attitudes toward and fears about their money, give it power—and the ability to wreak havoc on the most important relationships in their lives.

By now you probably realize that you are in a relationship with money, whether you think about it in these terms or not. Money is very often a third party in every relationship, the silent partner you set a place for every night at your dinner table. And just like the other important relationships in your life, you can't ignore it. This relationship needs work and attention to make it successful. How do I do this? you might ask.

You have to take actions with money that will create possibilities rather than destroy them, actions that will help you feel secure rather than afraid. Most of all, you have to take actions that will make you feel that you are loved unconditionally—for who you are, not for what you have—and that you can offer unconditional love to others. I have said it before, and I'll say it again: People first, then money.

But just because people come first doesn't mean money has no relevance whatsoever when it comes to love. Think of all the kinds of intimacy there are in the world—physical, emotional, domestic, etc. Of all these, financial intimacy is perhaps the hardest to achieve. Money is a loaded subject for almost all of us; everyone needs money, and money, whether you acknowledge this fact or not, holds great and far-reaching power over our lives. And yet we each have different and often clashing attitudes toward this important topic.

If you and your loved one haven't walked carefully and honestly through all the money issues that might come up in your relationship, I can promise you that money will one day become an obstacle in your relationship. Why? Because the nature of life is that people and things change. And any kind of change is a potential minefield. You change, your partner changes, and your money changes—it may grow or it may fail to grow. As we get older, our ideas about money change—as do our obligations. Not one of us is the same financial being at age 20 or 30 as we are at age 40 or 50, when we begin to see retirement—and even mortality—on the horizon.

The following questions and answers aren't meant to scare you away from making a commitment with the person you love. Rather, they are meant to demonstrate just how solemn and important—and sacred—lifetime commitments really are.

EMOTIONS AND MONEY

Are people really that different when it comes to dealing with money?

Yes. This can be very hard to understand and see clearly ahead of time, and it can be very painful to discover after you've made a commitment. Consider how you handle your money on your own, right now. You worry, sure, and maybe sometimes you spend money you shouldn't. You splurge on gifts for yourself and others, particularly around holidays, and occasionally you let your bills pile up. But when someone else, a fiancé or a spouse, has a stake in your money and you have a stake in theirs, sloppy habits or thoughtless spending or even incompatible views on how to manage money can strike at the core of how safe and secure you feel in your relationship.

Can you give me an example of how different attitudes toward money can be potentially damaging to my relationship?

Think about it. Every day, probably without realizing it, you see how the person you love acts with, and reacts to, money. You see the big things, like debt, and the little things, like the man who has to have every high-tech gadget out there, the woman who loves to buy shoes. Believe me, if these things, big or little, irk you now, they will irk you a lot more over time. At first you ignore what you don't like, probably in a much more forgiving way than you would other bad habits. Money is at once too small a subject for confrontations ("I don't want it to seem like I don't trust the guy I love!") and too great a subject, so you don't talk about it. By doing this, you are giving money the ultimate power: the power of silence.

What are the most common problems with money that couples come up against?

Most couples *think* they have problems with money for one or more of the following reasons: one partner spends too much while the other won't spend at all; one partner refuses to deal with money while the other deals only with money; one partner couldn't care less about money while the other cares only about money; one partner has too much money while the other has too little money. Sound familiar?

In my experience, however, I've found that so-called money problems usually have very little to do with money alone. They have more to do with how our self-worth compares to our net worth. We have been taught all our lives to see money as a kind of report card that tells us how we're doing. We measure our self-worth by how much we have in the bank, what clothes we wear, what cars we drive, which schools we send our kids to, our job titles, and so on—and not by our thoughts, feelings, and deeds. We seem to value the financial results of our actions more than the actions themselves and their effects on other people. This is especially true if we have come to believe, as so many of us have, that money is synonymous with security, that money and only money will ensure that we are taken care of and safe. And when our perceptions and priorities are skewed, when we put money before people, *that* is what causes problems in relationships.

What sorts of financial questions should my fiancé and I be asking each other before we get married?

Open up an honest dialogue as soon as you can. Don't just ask (or think to yourself), "Who's going to pay for what?" though that's an important question we'll get to later. You and your fiancé must ask—and answer—each other in a rational, candid way about money matters such as how you spend, how you save, how you invest, how well you share, and what your long-term plans are.

What if my future spouse's attitude toward money is very different fom mine? Do you believe that people can change their money habits just by talking about them? Yes, I think they can. Once you open the dialogue, you will be better able to see from your partner's perspective, and better able to act out of compassion for your partner's fears and concerns. Maybe the changes won't come all at once, but when people open up about money, they can work together toward a financial relationship that satisfies both parties. If you can state clearly and honestly what you find problematic or troubling about the way your loved one deals with money—or doesn't deal with it—then at least your perspective is out in the open. Remember, most changes that are worthwhile come not at once but over time, as you initiate a chain of actions. Make sure you promise each other to keep this dialogue about money open.

My fiancé always ends up getting angry when we talk about money. Our discussion starts off fine, then goes downhill.
The *way* you talk about money—your expression, your tone of voice, your timing—can be as important as what you are actually saying. Remember, money is an intimate subject for most people, sometimes more intimate than sex or religion, and when you talk about it, you must do it from an understanding and compassionate place, not from a blaming, or angry, or fearful place. When your fiancé gets angry talking about money,

that itself is a very important expression of his feelings about money. If you love him, you should try to take care of those feelings! And consider how his family might have raised him to look at money, too.

What does someone's family have to do with his or her feelings about money?
The way people are raised has a huge impact on how they deal—or don't deal—with money. The odds that you and your fiancé come from identical backgrounds as far as finances are concerned are pretty slim. I'm not talking about how much money your partner's family had when he was growing up, I'm talking about how the subject of money was treated. Were finances talked about openly? Secretly? Not at all? Was his mother a penny-pincher? Did his father splurge on trips and cars? Did they pretend they had money when in fact they didn't? Does your partner feel embarrassed about his or her economic background? Get all this stuff out in the open before you walk down the aisle. Talk about your past and about your future. Talk about the image each of you had of yourself as a kid and about the possibility of having your own kids, and about what's going to happen to your parents when they get older and can't take care of themselves. Get to know the person you're going to marry in a financial way, and you will know him better than you ever imagined. Remember, you and your partner will be handling the financial ups and downs of life, the boom times and the cautious times, together.

My fiancé is very frugal, and I tend to be an impulsive spender. Is there any hope for us in the long run?
Of course there is. Again, I'm asking you two to get all this out in the open before you walk down the aisle, and to try to understand the way your partner treats money from his or her

point of view. This will help you both compromise on issues of money management. For example, penny-pinchers are not necessarily Scrooges. Most of them are simply afraid of losing what they have; they think that there isn't enough money to go around. A spendthrift, on the other hand, may be using money to make up for low self-esteem or self-worth. There's always a reason someone actively goes about making his or her affairs chaotic. In the extreme case of a gambler, the damage may call for professional help, such as therapy or a 12-step program. The important thing is to talk about the different ways the two of you treat money. Silence will only prolong and worsen misunderstandings that can eventually damage your relationship.

I'm getting married in three months. Can you give me some examples of the money issues my fiancé and I should discuss before our wedding?

Absolutely. Let's begin with financial responsibility. Who is going to be doing the bookkeeping and the bill-paying in your household? Do you agree about your responsibilities, if any, toward your respective families? If applicable, are relations with ex-spouses (and children from a former marriage) clearly defined? What happens if one of you gets a great job offer that requires you to move—whose job takes precedence in this situation? If you have children, what happens if one of you wants to stay home with them? Do you feel the same way about the financial aspects of child-rearing, such as the costs of private versus public schools? Does one of you have trouble with debt, or a student loan that hasn't been paid off, or a lousy credit report? Are you going to keep some, or all, of your money separate? And even though it may seem a very long way away, you should begin talking about retirement. If you don't start thinking and talking about these questions before you get married, they are liable to be sticking points somewhere along the line. I strongly advise you to clear the air before rather than after your marriage. And even if you can't come to any final agreements, your relationship will be closer if you've at least talked out some of your concerns.

In addition to financial responsibilities, is there any other money issue we should discuss before we get married?

Yes. There is one more subject you and your partner must discuss to ensure your emotional and financial wealth in the years to come, and that is investing. Ask yourself and your partner these questions: How do you feel about saving for the future? Are you committed to investing for tomorrow? Do you agree that money you've saved shouldn't be touched, or would one of you be willing to take that money and use it for a luxury such as a vacation, or a hot tub, or a DVD player? Are your investment styles in sync?

What do you mean by investment styles being in sync?

I mean that every individual has a different tolerance for risk. Some people are very conservative when it comes to investing their money. They want steady growth over the years and a consistent income. Other people are willing to accept possible short-term losses on an investment that promises greater returns in the long run. Still others are willing to invest in something that looks risky because it might pay off big time. But far too many people haven't the slightest idea of how much risk they or their partners are willing to take with their money. Please make sure that you and your partner get this topic out into the open and talk about how much risk you are willing to take with your shared wealth before you embark on a life together.

Living Together

I am about to move in with my boyfriend of five years.
Do I need to prepare myself financially for living with
someone when we're not married?
Today, many couples—young couples just starting out, older
couples who, for various reasons, prefer not to marry, and same-
sex couples—are living together, and buying property together,
and need some of the same kinds of protection that married
couples do. When you're in love with someone and fantasizing
about your new life with him or her, you are probably not
thinking all that clearly about tomorrow. But this is a time when
you should be thinking seriously about your financial future,
especially since when you live with someone without the benefit of marriage, you have very little of the legal protection married couples have if and when it comes to dividing up assets.

Now, I know that the reason you are not getting married in
the first place may be that you don't like the idea of being
bound by a legal contract of any kind. Or you think marriage
is just a silly formality. Or you were married once before and
you got burned, and you don't want to make the same mistake
again. But whatever your reasons for not getting married are,
you should be aware that you may be leaving yourself vulnerable in a legal sense.

How am I vulnerable if I live with someone without
some kind of contract?
Consider some of the issues that typically come up when
people who have been living together for a long time call it
quits or when one of them dies. For example, what if you have

9

been depending on your partner financially for a couple of years? If you break up, you have no right to keep getting financial support, and you also have no right to share in any of the assets your partner may have accumulated during the years you lived together.

Remember the Lee Marvin case in California, in which the actor's longtime live-in companion sued him for "palimony"? She based her lawsuit on her claim that Lee Marvin had promised that he would support her for the rest of her life and that the assets that they each accumulated during their relationship belonged to both of them. But when two people get really mad at each other, do you think one or the other will go out of his way to remind the other one of the terms of their agreement? Human nature doesn't work that way.

What if you made a significant gift to your partner, expecting that you'd be together forever, and you now regret giving that gift? What if your partner gets sick, so sick he can't make medical decisions for himself? You remember that when you and your partner talked about this, he was very firm about not wanting any extraordinary medical measures taken in this situation. Well, guess what? Your partner's sister wants to have him hooked up to a ventilator, and you have no legal right to keep her from doing so. What if you and your partner agreed that you would inherit each other's estates in the event either of you died? You shook hands on it, and you probably assumed that was all there was to that. Guess what? In the eyes of the court, you are not your partner's legal heir, as you would have been if you were married.

Are there any other problems people can get into without a legal and enforceable agreement?

Yes. To take a typical example, what if you and your partner decide to buy a house together? If your partner is kicking in more than you are, it may seem to make sense to have the property held solely in his name. Then you break up, and guess who gets the house? What if both names are on the title even though you contributed more for the down payment, never discussing whether or not you'd get reimbursed for your excess contribution? Or what if you assume you have the rights of joint tenancy with your partner? This means that if he dies, 100 percent of the house will go to you, the surviving partner. But when your partner dies, you discover that you misread the title and that instead of being a joint tenant, you are a tenant-in-common. This means that your partner's share of the house goes directly to his estate. What if he left his estate to his younger brother, the one who's been in jail? By law, this guy can move in with you.

Is there any way I can protect myself financially while my partner and I are living together?

Yes. Before we get into cohabitation agreements, there are a few things you should do just to be on the safe side. For one thing, you should make all your financial expectations (and intentions) very clear to your partner. If you give him $500 for his birthday, write the word "gift" on the check so that in the worst case scenario, the court will not be able to view this check as evidence of a promise you made to support your partner. If it is a loan that you expect to be repaid, write "loan" on the check. Never put money in a joint account just because you think it will add trust or convenience to your relationship, and don't put both names on a title unless you are truly *joint* owners, by which I mean fifty-fifty.

Why do you advise against putting my partner's name on my accounts?

Because if someone ever filed a palimony lawsuit against you, a joint account or joint ownership of property could be seen by the court as powerful evidence of an understanding between you and your partner to share everything. In some states, including California, the courts make decisions on the validity of cohabitation agreements if there seemed to be an "implied" agreement between the two partners, whereas in other states, a written agreement is required.

My boyfriend and I are about to move in together and probably will get married. Should we merge our money or keep separate accounts?

You'll definitely want to keep separate accounts, though you may also want to merge some of your money for common expenses. I'd advise you to keep separate accounts for your individual personal expenses. You wouldn't give up your personal identity for your boyfriend, and you shouldn't surrender your financial identity to him, either. Your money is an integral part of you, just as your boyfriend's money is an integral part of him. When you marry or live together, you're creating a new, third entity—a partnership—that deserves a bank account of its own. You each have a right to autonomy when it comes to your money, and the right to decide how and when to spend the money you've earned.

What about credit cards?

You should keep separate credit cards as well, so as to establish your own financial identity in the world of credit, now and for whenever you may want it later.

What sort of account do you suggest my fiancé and I open jointly?

For as little as $1,000, you and your boyfriend can open a money market account with a good mutual funds company, tap into it every month for your joint expenses, and also invest sums of money so they can begin to grow for your future to-gether. Money coming in and growing is the way to nurture and share in tomorrow's fortunes together. Money market accounts pay higher interest rates than savings accounts, and you can usually write checks against them.

How should we determine who contributes what to cover our monthly expenses?

Let's say your joint expenses for living together will be around $3,000 a month. (When you're calculating your monthly expenses, always add an extra 10 percent; we always underestimate how much we spend to live, and you want to build this account up in case of unexpected expenses.) Based on your current incomes, you've agreed that your boyfriend will kick in $2,000 a month, and your contribution will be $1,500 a month. Of that total, $3,500, use $3,000 to pay your bills and $500 to invest in the future. And since you're both contributing what you can, in good faith you should share *equally*—not in proportion to what you put in —in the future growth of that $500 per month. You're partners, after all, and you should have a stake in each other's future, not just this month's bills.

COHABITATION AGREEMENTS

How can I avoid legal and financial complications if I am planning to live with someone?

There is a very good way. I suggest that you and your partner draw up a cohabitation agreement. This is simply a written agreement that governs all your rights and obligations with respect to finances and separate property, as well as any other expectations that either of you might have regarding your financial situation before you move in together. If you find out that you and your partner have different expectations about finances, better that you find this out now rather than later!

Can we just draft this agreement on my computer, or does it have to be prepared by an attorney?

Of course you can draft the agreement on your computer. Any written agreement is better than none at all. But ideally you each would have an attorney review it, since attorneys can identify any pitfalls or loopholes.

Do we each have to have our own attorney?

Yes, for the same reason I advise that you do when you are drawing up a prenuptial agreement (more about these later). If your cohabitation agreement should ever come into question, the court might question its validity if it thought that either one of you had not been fairly represented by counsel. This is especially true if a lot of money is at stake.

Do courts really honor cohabitation agreements?

Almost every state in the union does, so long as it is in writing. Many states will consider oral or implied agreements, but since memories often differ in the dissolution of a relationship, it can be very hard to prove an oral agreement.

What is an implied agreement?

The court defines an implied agreement as a pattern of actions or conduct that suggests an unspoken understanding between the two parties in question. Such actions or conduct may include owning joint property, or opening a shared checking or savings account, or a history of one partner working and the other one staying at home. If you have been financially supporting the woman you live with for some time and the two of you break up, a jury could find that the two of you had an "understanding" that this state of affairs would continue indefinitely—even if, in your mind, no such understanding even existed!

How about an oral versus a written agreement?

An oral agreement is just what it sounds like—an actual exchange of spoken words, with clear expressions of agreement. Better have it on paper is my advice! Written agreements are far superior to oral and implied agreements. They are much more specific, and they provide a lot more peace of mind. In the worst-case scenario, they will clarify for a jury just what was in both your minds when you drew up the agreement in the first place. And, even better, they provide you and the person you love a chance to go over your finances with a fine-tooth comb, thus eliminating possible future areas of disagreement or misunderstanding.

SAME-SEX COHABITATION

What's the difference between a cohabitation agreement in a same-sex relationship versus a cohabitation agreement in a heterosexual one?

Legally, there's no difference, but in practice there may be a big difference. Whether you're gay or straight, living together doesn't provide much of a legal structure for the rights and obligations of the parties involved unless you've entered into an agreement of some kind. But in this country marriage isn't an option for same-sex partners. So it's up to you and your partner to define the terms of your agreement. Legally, there's no difference between straight couples living together and gay or lesbian couples who choose to share a house. But in some parts of the country, a gay partner may find it exceedingly difficult to enforce the terms of an oral or an implied cohabitation agreement in court. People's ideas of morality come in here, since some jurors may not look kindly or compassionately on your relationship. In addition, many same-sex partners may not have given much thought to long-term financial issues, so it is particularly important in their case to have sat down and really hashed out their intentions.

What should we do to state our intentions clearly?

Put them in writing. There are several excellent books to help you get started (see Resources) and if you have significant assets, you should consult a qualified attorney. I know a gay couple who went so far as to videotape their intentions in front of a lawyer, just to make sure that no one in either of their families could challenge the rights that each partner had given to the other.

I am in a same-sex relationship, and my partner and I own property together. What happens in the event we break up?

If the property is held jointly, either party can petition the court to sell the property and divide the proceeds of the sale according to the terms of their agreement. The partners can also try to reach an amicable agreement between themselves by putting the property on the market and dividing the proceeds of the sale, or one partner can buy out the other's share.

My partner's name is on the title of the house we are living in together, but I have been paying the mortgage. Now we are breaking up. Do I have any rights to the property?

The property will go to the partner who holds title, or whose name is on the account, unless the unnamed party can claim that he or she had an agreement with the partner to share the asset. (In some states, only written agreements can supercede the title.) The dispute will be resolved in the ordinary "business" division of the local court, rather than the family law division, and contract law rather than family law will apply.

If my partner and I haven't bought property together, are we still financially obligated toward each other in some way?

In just about every state, contracts between unmarried couples—including same-sex couples—are legally binding. It's better for the contracts to be in writing, since proving a contract is pretty hard to do if it isn't written down, and oral contracts are rarely enforced. But if you strongly believe that you and your partner had a firm contract and you can afford to fight for your rights in court, you may be able to prove your case. And if your partner thinks you made such an agreement, and you happen to disagree, you could still find yourself faced with a legal claim.

My partner and I are gay. Can we enter into a common-law marriage?

No. Common-law marriages don't apply to same-sex couples.

Since my partner and I can't marry anyway, it can't be all that practical or important for us to have all of these agreements, right?

If anything, it is even more important! As same-sex partners, you do not have the legal options that marriage automatically confers, so you have to create these legal safeguards for yourselves. Remember, you cannot rely on a family court to protect you or assist in dividing up your property if you separate; there is no jurisdiction in this country that will automatically recognize your inheritance rights. If you have children, you cannot collect child support and you cannot appeal to the judicial system for custody or visitation (except in those few places where a same-sex partner can adopt his or her partner's children). Even more than heterosexual couples—who can, after all, get married in a pinch if a life-altering event looms—gay couples in serious relationships should have some or all of the following: wills, health-care proxies, durable powers of attorney, adoption and/or custody agreements, and written agreements about the disposal of joint property. Though some of these may not be fully enforceable in many jurisdictions, they do provide a framework to guide your actions at times when you may be emotionally unprepared to make sound, fair decisions.

PRENUPTIAL AGREEMENTS

What exactly is a prenuptial agreement?

A prenuptial—or premarital or antemarital—agreement is a legal contract a couple enters into before marriage that states how the couple's assets, as well as their debts, are to be divided in case of a divorce. The pre-nup can also spell out certain expectations each partner brings to a marriage, i.e., who will work, who will stay at home with the children, and various inheritance rights. Think of it as the best way to ensure the protection of your future.

I thought pre-nups were just for rich people.

You are not alone in thinking that. It's true that years ago, pre-nups were for those who had considerable wealth they wanted to protect. Even today we tend to read about pre-nups in terms of movie stars, or the very rich, who are trying to protect their enormous assets. And often, when I bring up the subject with my clients, they burst out laughing. "Why do I need a pre-nup?" they ask. "I'm not rich!" or "I have barely any assets to my name." But these are words of poverty. Pre-nups have less to do with your financial situation today than they do with your future. Even people who have very few assets enter into pre-nups in order to protect what they might have tomorrow, to protect themselves against debtors if a would-be spouse is irresponsible with his or her finances, and ultimately, to protect themselves, no matter what happens, forever.

I'm still not convinced I need a pre-nup. Can you give me some examples of situations in which someone would want to have one?

Yes. Here are some scenarios in which pre-nups come into play. You and your spouse-to-be both work, and you might want to keep future earnings or stock options separate. Or you have previously been through a terrible divorce, and you know very well what can happen and how painful and divisive (not to mention expensive) it can be to decide who is going to get what. You want to make absolutely sure that you never have to go through that again. Or you inherited an extensive portfolio from your parents, a portfolio that may take you—and possibly your spouse—a lot of time and effort to manage. You will both reap the rewards during your marriage. Even so, you want to make sure that this portfolio and its growth remain in your name alone should the marriage dissolve.

I know that one day I'm going to inherit my parents' vacation home. Since my folks no longer use the house very much, my fiancé and I have begun using it every weekend and are full of plans to fix it up together. Still,

*this house has been in my family for several genera-
tions, and I want to make sure it remains in my family.
Is this something a pre-nup could cover?*
It certainly is, and I think it's a very good idea. A pre-nup is a
good idea anytime you want to make sure that any kind of asset—whether property, or equity, or securities, or a retirement
plan—is protected.

*Isn't it kind of insulting to tell the guy I'm going to
marry that I want a pre-nup? Doesn't that imply to him
that I already don't have much confidence in our future
together?*
That's certainly the myth—that bringing up the subject of pre-
nups will cause arguing and suspicion and disagreements. But
in reality, it's a way of bringing to the surface your most intimate concerns abut money, and security, and all the other
unknowns of the future. I don't think it's a sign of greed, or
weakness, or fear, or suspicion, to desire reassurance that you
both will be safe, whatever happens in the future. I happen to
think that signing a pre-nup is a great idea, that it's a sign of
wisdom and responsibility. After all, a pre-nup says that whatever you came into this relationship with, and whatever you
might bring to it, you will get to leave with. In my experience,
talking honestly about money and assets and your future can
bring partners closer together in ways they can only guess at
until they do it.

*Okay, you've convinced me. How do I go about getting
a prenuptial agreement drawn up?*
One thing you *don't* want to do is rely on one of the plethora
of "how-to" CD-ROMs for creating your own prenuptial
agreement. In my opinion, pre-nups are much too important
to rely on the latest computer software, no matter how good it

is, or how good your intentions (and your desire to save a buck) are. Computer programs and resource books can certainly be a good starting point, and they might also give you some good ideas, but I would never favor them over what a good attorney can draft according to the laws of your state. Do-it-yourselfers beware!

The first thing I advise is for each of you to consult a lawyer—and not the same lawyer, either!—to make sure that the final agreement the two of you have reached together works for both of you. This may feel a little strange, as though you are taking sides already, but it is best for you each to have separate legal representation.

Are we required by law to have separate lawyers?

Yes, in some states, separate representation is actually required for the agreement to be valid. But even where it isn't required by law, I would strongly advise that you have separate attorneys. That way, you'll have a chance to air your concerns privately. Moreover, if the pre-nup should ever come into play, neither of you can say that you did not know what you were signing or did not understand the agreement, or that one or the other was unfairly represented by counsel. You should have your lawyers sign the agreement as well, to show that they both have reviewed it carefully.

How should I prepare for this meeting? What are the lawyers who are drawing up my pre-nup on the look-out for?

Several things. First of all, it is very important that you and your partner disclose to each other all your assets and liabilities, and agree to enter into this agreement freely and without any undue coercion. Courts can be very sensitive to this, and all of us have read about pre-nups later being overturned be-

cause one party claimed he or she was pressured into signing his or her name. Also, the terms of the pre-nup must be
fair.

What does "fair" mean in this context?
In this context, "fair" means that the pre-nup agreement takes
into account your age, your partner's age, your state of health,
your job, your income, your standard of living, your family responsibilities, if applicable, and your preexisting assets, whether
they include property, or an investment portfolio, or an insurance policy. You and your partner must show evidence that
you understand the extent of each other's assets and income.
Sometimes, your lawyer will suggest that you or your partner
bring copies of your recent tax returns, or your monthly statements from a brokerage firm, or any other financial information that could affect the pre-nup. Full disclosure of both your
and your partner's assets is essential. Also, you must both show
that you fully understand the legal and financial consequences
of this arrangement. If a court later deems the agreement unfair, it can be thrown out!

Do I need to disclose everything I have in the pre-nup?
Yes. It is important that you disclose it all—your assets, your
debts, your income, your expenses, and anything else that will
affect the value of your estate, now or in the future.

Does a pre-nup deal exclusively with asset ownership?
No. Other items such as debt, or future stock options, or retirement benefits, can be designated in the agreement. There
have been pre-nups that cover everything from who will get
the baseball season tickets to who has to feed the dog. Almost
anything can be covered as long as it does not violate public
policy.

What, exactly, is the definition of property?

In most courts of law, property includes everything from your old coin collection to your retirement funds. It also includes debts, patents, intellectual property (such as novels and screenplays), artwork—you name it. When it comes to the definition of "property," feel free to expand your thoughts to go way beyond such things as your car, your boat, your furniture, your book or music royalties, your jewelry, or your house. Property basically includes everything you can think of.

Is there anything that can't be put in a pre-nup?

As long as it is legal, you can basically put in whatever financial terms you like, though issues of child custody and child support cannot be put in a pre-nup. Of course contracts that appear to anticipate illegal actions (such as gambling, or even murder!) are not enforceable, and the same goes for pre-nups that force one or the other partner into obligatory sexual duties. Courts really don't want to get into that, for obvious reasons. Any agreement that would leave a spouse totally destitute or a ward of the state is also unenforceable.

Can the pre-nup include our wills?

No. A pre-nup only covers what happens in the event of a dissolution, not a death. Another thing to bear in mind: Each of you can always change your will unilaterally.

This all sounds so formal and strange. Are you sure it's a good idea for my fiancé and me?

I would stake my future and yours on it. Remember that entering into a pre-nup is an act of love and respect, not an act of pessimism or suspicion. So many people get the idea into their heads that this document is unromantic, or that it means their partner is leery of their intentions. All I can do is tell you that from my experience, this is far from the truth. All of my clients who have asked for a prenuptial agreement have been motivated by love and respect for their own and their partner's security, not by disrespect or lack of trust. Furthermore, when I think of couples I've worked with in which the partners did not mind signing a prenuptial agreement—who in fact were happy to do so—not only are those couples still together today, but many of them have actually asked years afterward for the prenuptial to be rescinded in order to give their partners full rights to everything they have. For those couples in which one partner opposed the idea from the start, the exact opposite is all too often true: Many of them ended up either separated or divorced. My advice is for you to let your beloved know that this is something that is important to you, and that you strongly believe in it. In my opinion, if someone really loves you, he or she will want to be protected and to feel safe, and should be more than happy to sign.

Do judges really pay attention to pre-nups? If they don't, is it really worth making my fiancé sign one?
Until recently, judges were not all that favorably inclined toward pre-nups. Years ago, many states did practically everything they could to discourage divorce. They did not want to honor pre-nups, because the thinking was that pre-nups somehow planted the idea of divorce in people's heads before they even walked down the aisle. Well, times have changed, and these days most judges have come to recognize that in many cases, people are better off if they do get divorced—and if they do, they're better off having signed a pre-nup. So now, generally speaking, the courts enforce these agreements. However, they will not honor the contract if the court feels that it gave one spouse a powerful incentive to end the marriage, for they see this kind of a contract as one that promotes divorce—which they still don't

look favorably upon. Furthermore, the pre-nup won't be enforced it it's viewed as a contract to evade creditors illegally, or if the court believes that one party was intimidated into signing.

Do all 50 states recognize pre-nups?

Yes. There is a nationwide Uniform Prenuptial Agreement Act (UPAA), although the particular laws of each state may differ as to the conditions for enforcing a pre-nup.

After we've met with both our lawyers, then what happens?

Pre-nups must be put in writing, and signed by both parties and both attorneys. If for some reason you have chosen not to retain an individual attorney to represent your interests, you should at least hire one to review the contract and advise you about its implications before you sign it. These contracts can be fairly complicated, and you want to make sure that each of you knows exactly what you are signing.

Where and when should the agreement be signed?

I will tell you this much: Don't sign it on the way to the wedding! Remember that courts are very sensitive to the emotional states of both people signing, and they will throw out your pre-nup later if they feel that either party was under duress while signing, or that the parties did not have ample time to think about it, or to seek adequate professional help. Make sure that you draw up your agreement under the most normal circumstances you can think of, which simply means that you and your partner signed the pre-nup of your own free wills and without any kind of coercion.

Do pre-nups have to be witnessed and/or notarized in order to be valid?

Rules vary from state to state. For example, in New York, a pre-nup must be notarized to be valid, but in some states neither witnesses nor notaries are necessary. Your attorney(s) will know the requirements in your state.

How much does it cost to draft a pre-nup?

In some cases, only a couple hundred dollars—not very much when you consider how much a bitter divorce can cost—and in other cases as much as several thousand dollars. After all, it's not unusual for some divorces that end up in court to cost tens of thousands of dollars, affect children in the most negative possible way, and take years to resolve. When you think of what the future could bring, the pre-nup is a very good investment.

What if we want to make some changes after the contract is drawn up and signed?

This isn't a problem. You basically follow the same procedure you followed when you had the contract drawn up in the first place. Have the agreement witnessed and notarized, if necessary, and state expressly whether you're replacing the earlier document with this one or simply emending certain terms listed in the previous agreement. If you draft an agreement *after* you are married, this is technically known as a postnuptial agreement.

We've been married for over 20 years and so much about our financial situation has changed since we first drew up our prenuptial agreement. Should we change the pre-nup or should we just dissolve it? It seems like there's no reason to have one anymore.

The truth is, I don't think you should ever dissolve your pre-nup. Changes in your or your partner's financial status, which may strike you as a possible motivation to change or abandon the pre-nup, should be accounted for in the original document *if* it was drawn up correctly—and that's admittedly a big if. The primary reason to have a pre-nup has more to do with having the peace of mind that both you and your spouse will be protected, whatever may come. If your agreement was drafted thoughtfully and with that goal in mind, then changing the document should not be necessary. "Whatever may come" is the key phrase here—we never know what the future holds for us, good or bad, so why risk exposing ourselves by dissolving an agreement that's all about protection? If you never need to use it, all the better. It'll just sit in its file and grow happily obsolete.

I'm a widow with three children from a previous marriage, and I am getting married again next spring. Should I get a pre-nup?
Definitely, if only to protect your children's futures. If you want your children to inherit your property, you should get a pre-nup drawn up today. Otherwise, your new husband will have certain rights to at least a portion of your assets.

Given that second marriages are so very common today, pre-nups are becoming popular among couples who want to make sure to put into writing the assets they want to keep safe for their children from earlier marriages. This is crucial particularly if you are a widow (or widower) with children, and you want to protect their father's (or mother's) money for them before you remarry. Or if you are remarrying and don't want your grown children to be suspicious or resentful of a new stepparent, a pre-nup will demonstrate to them that assets due to go to them one day will in fact do so.

PRE-NUPS AND DEBT

What's the connection between pre-nups and debt, present and future?

In most cases, when you go into a marriage, you are not responsible for any debts that your partner incurred before the marriage. You will, however, be responsible for any debts incurred by your partner while you are married. Clearly, if you have a joint credit card and it's issued in both your names, you are both responsible.

But what happens if the credit card is issued only in my spouse's name?

This is a lot trickier. Let's consider those credit cards that your spouse was issued in his or her name alone, for his or her own purposes. What if your partner runs up a lot of debt, then you get divorced, and after the divorce he or she declares bankruptcy? Even though your name was not on the credit card, the company has the legal right to come after you for that money. Why? Because if he or she checked "married" in the box next to marital status on the application, then in very fine print (of course), the application stated that the spouse is also responsible for the debt unless otherwise noted.

So my pre-nup gives me no protection against most of my partner's debts?

In some states, you can protect yourself by having your lawyer draw up a pre-nup that specifies which debts you will not be responsible for. For example, you could state that any credit cards in your spouse's name alone are not your responsibility.

This option, however, may not be available to you in your particular state. Check the laws to see if it is possible to protect yourself by sending a copy of your prenuptial agreement to all pertinent credit card companies, including those with which you set up new accounts.

COMMON-LAW MARRIAGES

What exactly is a common-law marriage?
Some states in this country—currently there are 11, plus the District of Columbia—recognize what is known as a "common-law" marriage. In this situation, a man and a woman who have lived together for a certain amount of time, and who think of themselves and present themselves to the public as man and wife, are considered by the state in which they live to be married.

Do they need a marriage license or a wedding ceremony?
No. The laws don't require either one. But since the marriage is not formally recorded anywhere, the burden of proof is on the couple if the relationship ever comes into question. At that point, the man and the woman have to prove that they live together as man and wife and that they present themselves publicly as married.

What do you need to prove that you are in a common-law marriage?
The laws differ from state to state. In general, a couple must prove they have the mental capacity to marry, and they must have lived together under one roof for a significant period of

time (this period of time is not defined in any state). They should share the same last name, and refer to each other as "my wife" and "my husband," and file joint tax returns. Their friends and acquaintances must also consider them to be married.

If you are in a common-law marriage and it breaks up, do you file for divorce the same way you would if you had had a formal marriage ceremony?
Yes.

What if both of us agree that we were not involved in a common-law marriage after all? Do we have to go through the courts to get a divorce?
No. If you and your partner live in a state that acknowledges common-law marriage and you decide to end your relationship, and you both agree that you do not have a common-law marriage, then you do not have to go to court to get a formal divorce. If there's a dispute about this between the two of you, a judge will have to step in and resolve it.

Do marital rights automatically accrue to a person who lives with you as a spouse over a long period of time?
Only if you live in states that honor common-law marriages. It comes as a big surprise to a lot of people, but in many states you can hold yourself out as husband and wife, file joint returns, and so on, but if you're not married you get nothing if your partner dies or leaves. It's even possible that if someone were in an intensive care unit, his or her partner wouldn't be allowed in in a *non*–common-law state—because he or she would not be considered "next of kin." Establishing a durable power of attorney for health care ("durable" because it remains

in effect even if you become incapacitated) is the only way to protect yourself against this possibility and it is a crucial consideration for unmarried partners.

What states currently recognize common-law marriages?

In no particular order, the states are Oklahoma, Pennsylvania, Rhode Island, Alabama, Colorado, Iowa, Kansas, South Carolina, Texas, Utah, and Montana, as well as the District of Columbia, and for inheritance purposes only, New Hampshire.

MARRIAGE AND MONEY

What are my obligations to my wife, financially speaking, now that we are married?

After you and your wife have obtained and signed your marriage license, and taken various blood tests to prove that neither of you is carrying any diseases, you and she have entered into a legal contract with each other. What are some of the conditions of this contract? First of all, according to the statutes in most states, each of you is obligated to support the other financially. Husband and wife agree to provide each other "obligations of mutual respect, fidelity, and support." This applies if a spouse becomes ill or loses—or quits—a job.

I'm not going to be bringing in any income, since I work at home taking care of our new baby. Does this mean I'm breaking the contract?

The laws of most states don't specify how much support a spouse has to provide or what form that support must take. And it's very likely that your state views what you plan to do as "contributing financially" to your marriage, since in fact, you very much are!

What are some other terms of the marital contract?

Some of the other terms of the marriage contract may include a legal obligation to share your estate with your spouse when you die. Many states allow a spouse to take what is known as a forced share, the amount any spouse is entitled to by law, regardless of the other spouse's wishes. The amount varies from state to state, but it can be up to one-third of the estate. You have the right to file your tax returns jointly. You have the right to retirement and government benefits based on your partner's contributions—disability, income from various pensions, and Social Security. In the event of a divorce, you have the right to claim a share of whatever property and income you and your husband accumulate during your marriage, and in some cases, you may be entitled to half of all combined assets. And you can make decisions about your spouse's medical care if he or she is not competent to make those decisions.

What about property that I acquired before the marriage? How is this regarded by the courts?

Property acquired before your marriage is generally known as separate property. It remains separate property as long as you keep it in your name alone and you spouse doesn't have any access to it or contribute to its maintenance. Even so, it never hurts to have all this detailed in the pre-nup. Problems can arise, however, if your partner contributes time and/or money to help maintain a premarital property, thus increasing its value. In some states, whether or not your partner contributes time and/or money to the asset, the appreciation of the property—that is to say, how much its value has risen—may be considered a joint asset in any case.

What if I'm left an inheritance or am given a gift by my parents after I am married? Is that property considered joint property?

If those funds were given specifically to you and you keep them in an account in your name only, or if you buy something with those funds in your name only, then in most states, they will remain your separate property. Please note, however, that the longer a marriage goes on, the more boundaries between a husband and wife's separate monies and property can blur. "Mine" and "yours" over time becomes "ours"—usually you don't even think about it! Say you buy some mutual funds, for example, and it's the most convenient thing at the time to name your spouse a joint owner. You may have just unwittingly converted your separate property to joint, marital, or in some states, community property. Where you want such assets to end up, or how they should be divided, should be spelled out clearly in the pre-nup.

What if I owned rental property before I was married and continue to earn from it during the marriage—is the rental income still considered my separate property?

Good question. In some states, if both you and your partner invest time and effort in the management of the property, the current income can be considered a joint asset, since it's the product of both your labor, rather than a passive solitary investment. If you use a management company, however, the rent is more often considered a separate asset. The laws on this vary widely from state to state, so check the law in your state.

My husband and I have been married only six months, and already we're squabbling about financial stuff. He

spends money on computer equipment. I spend money
on household things. He insists on paying the bills, then
he forgets about them, and sometimes we end up pay-
ing the same bill twice, or not at all. I feel as if an enor-
mous gap has opened up between us.

You're not alone. As I said at the beginning of this book, sharing finances with someone is no day at the beach. After all, all
your adult life you've been managing your own money your
own way, and now you're supposed to do it with another person? Not just the rent or the mortgage, but everything? It may
sound like a cliché, but merging your finances with another
person's means compromise. It means sometimes putting someone else's interests and needs ahead of your own.

This is why I always suggest talking about these issues before you get married rather than waiting until you are married
to be surprised by your partner's financial habits or behavior.
Remember, no two partners are exactly alike, and no two couples manage their finances in quite the same way. For example,
there is nothing more frustrating, if you're sharing a joint checking account, than to pay the bills and then have the phone ring
off the hook because the checks bounced when, according
to your figures, there should have been more than enough
money in the account to pay for everything. You call up the
bank, only to find out that the love of your life forgot to deposit your last paycheck, or perhaps forgot to record a couple
of checks he wrote, or made a large cash withdrawal from the
ATM and spent it all without ever saying a word to you. Each
one of us has our own financial housekeeping preferences—
some of us balance the bank statement every month, some
never balance it. Some of us will pay the bills as soon as they
come in, while others have no problem being late every
month. But regardless of how you deal with your money, it is
essential that you work out a plan that will meet the needs of

both of you in handling the coming and the going of your money.

Can you give me some concrete ideas about how we can start handling our money together?
First things first. Even if only one of you does the actual book-keeping, you should both be familiar with everything there is to know about your money. You should both know the costs of food, clothing, and shelter. If you have children, you should both understand the children's expenses and how much their education is going to cost. This is the only way for you to be respectful of the money you have in common—and respectful and protective of each other, because it is unfair that the burden of bills falls on just one of you. Why not consider paying the bills together every month? If that doesn't work for you or makes you crazy, one of you might do it one month and the other the next, or switch every six months. But ideally, it's important that you both touch, know about, and deal with your money. It's also essential that you be honest about debts or ongoing financial obligations that either of you are committed to.

What about spending money? That's where my wife and I have the biggest arguments.
Spending and bookkeeping go hand in hand. You must sit down with each other and hash out certain financial realities. For example, how often will you get a new car? What about vacations? How much will the holiday season cost? Are you going to give any money to any charities? Bottom line: You must talk about and compromise on or agree on what you need, what you want, and what you can afford. You must have a vision for tomorrow, and a means of getting there. Remember—two people, contributing small sums of money over time, can

build up a fortune a whole lot faster than one person. Two people working at it together can make a mortgage vaporize. Two people can put their children through school. Two people, even if one of them doesn't work outside the home for money, can together create a life with greater depth and texture and richness than most of us can on our own. If you share joyously and willingly, if your commitment is financial as well as emotional, then your marriage will be a rich, happy place to inhabit.

Is there any advantage to trying to keep our monies separate by filing separate tax returns?
The answer in most cases is no. Filing separately can actually take away certain tax advantages that you gain when you file jointly. Even couples who are at each other's throats in the midst of a terrible divorce tend to file together as long as they can if it results in some sort of tax benefit! (Bear in mind, however, that in some states, California among them, an ex-spouse's tax return can be subpoenaed by the other party and used to determine adjustments in the amount of child or spousal support. A new spouse might want to keep his or her information out of the picture, and filing separately would achieve that—even though it usually costs more in taxes to do it that way.) The rules for this arena are subject to change, so if the amounts involved are significant, check with your accountant.

You mentioned debts earlier. Am I liable for the debts that my spouse incurred before we got married?
No. You don't marry debt. But as soon as you commingle your assets with your spouse's, any *joint* account you set up becomes fair game for prior creditors. You can get around this law in certain states by keeping or opening a bank account in your

own name, which creditors theoretically can't touch. Even so, the IRS has the power to put a lien on a refund due when you file a joint tax return. So your spouse's prior tax liens are the scariest debts to marry. Get this topic out in the open sooner rather than later!

Am I liable for debts incurred after our marriage that are only in my spouse's name?

You may be. It depends on where you live, but in most states, for all intents and purposes, you and your husband are financially responsible for each other. If your spouse can't pay his bills, creditors will always try to get you to pay, and you'll be the one who has to go to great lengths (and expense) to prove you're not liable.

What happens if my spouse files for bankruptcy?

The creditors may be able to come after you for the entire amount of the debts—even if your spouse is actually an ex-spouse by now—if you were legally married when the debts were in the process of piling up. If you are both liable for the debt, one spouse's discharge of the debt in bankruptcy court will not relieve the other spouse of the debt, which believe it or not, may show up as a flag on the "good" spouse's credit report. What this means is that if your ex-spouse claims bankruptcy, it may show up on your credit rating reports because you are also responsible for the debt that was accumulated in both, or either, of your names when you were legally married. Just because your ex got out of it does not mean you're in the clear, even if the debt was in his or her name alone while you were married.

COMMUNITY-PROPERTY STATES

I live in a community-property state. What exactly does community property mean?

Community-property states include Arizona, California, Idaho, Louisiana, Nevada, New Mexico, Texas, Washington, and Wisconsin. Community property is everything acquired during the marriage, regardless of whose funds or income were used, yours or your partner's. (The exceptions here include gifts, inheritances, or anything else agreed upon by both parties as not being community property, as well as any income generated by separate property.) When you acquire something that falls under the classification of community property, then it is considered to be owned equally by both of you. This is true of any debt you accumulate during your marriage, as well as property and other assets. If you wish to handle your property or acquisitions in another way, you can so specify in a pre-nup. In community-property states, all community property is divided equally upon dissolution of marriage.

Why do some people try to get their divorces to take place in community-property states?

Because when a marriage ends in a community-property state, all community property is divided up fifty-fifty. In non–community-property states, the court can divide the joint assets however the judge thinks is most fair, depending on the financial needs and abilities of the two parties.

Wait a minute. Does this mean that if I live in a community-property state, I'm responsible for the debts of my spouse?

The answer again is that your separate funds cannot be attached for any debts incurred by your spouse before the marriage. Nevertheless, creditors can come after your half of the community-property funds to pay for a debt that your spouse incurred before (or during) marriage. They can even attach your wages if they want—unless you specify otherwise in a pre-nup or deposit your wages in a separate account to which your spouse has no access whatsoever. If you live in a community-property state and you spouse comes into the relationship with sizable debt, you should discuss setting up a separate account for your wages. Again, please make sure that your prenuptial agreement states your intention to keep your earnings separate. If you don't like these rules, you might want to think twice about getting married!

If we draw up a pre-nup in one state and then we move to another state, what happens? Is it still valid?

You should have the original contract checked by a good attorney in the new state. If anything needs to be changed, your attorney in the new state can make those changes.

If we have a pre-nup and the way in which we decide to divide our property is different from that dictated by the laws of the state where we live, will our pre-nup stand?

In most cases, yes. If the contract is drawn up correctly, your agreement will allow you to modify or even wriggle out of the state property system, even if you live in a community-property state. Then you can implement an agreement that better suits your needs.

JOINT ACCOUNTS

My wife and I have decided to share our bills. Should we open a joint account of some kind?

In my opinion, a joint checking account or a money market fund with both of your names attached to it is essential, for the simple reason that you are not going to split the bills, but *share* them. You have decided to join your lives and therefore your money, and this account is symbolic of that union. Unless you want to start calculating who drinks more orange juice or uses more toothpaste, you must have a place to house the money you use to pay for those bills and items that you share.

Okay, I've done the calculations you suggested. Our expenses, including the additional 10 percent, come to around $4,000 a month. Now what?

Now you and your husband should prepare to contribute the exact same *percentage* of each of your salaries toward paying those bills. In this case, after taxes, retirement contributions, health insurance, etc., you take home $5,000 a month and your husband's take-home paycheck is around $3,000. Add the two take-home checks together. This comes to $8,000 ($5,000 plus $3,000). Now divide the total of your joint expenses, $4,000, by the total of your joint take-home checks ($4,000 divided by $8,000). This equals the percentage, 50 percent, of your take-home pay that each of you should contribute to your joint account—$2,500 for you; $1,500 for your husband. Again, you should each be contributing the same percentage of your take-home checks to support your lifestyle and to pay the bills you owe. Remember, the amounts do not have to be the same to make your contributions equal, only the percentages.

It doesn't seem fair that I have to contribute more just because I make more. Does this mean I have a bigger say in how we spend the money?
First, on a percentage basis, you are not contributing more; you and your husband are contributing the same *proportion* of your respective salaries to the joint account. Second, in most states, both parties' income is legally considered joint property, since the marriage is a financial as well as an emotional partnership, remember? And third, even though you are paid better than your husband, this does not mean you work any harder than he does, and therefore should have more power over your finances, or that you are entitled to more. The world, as most of us discovered when we were children, is seldom a fair place—if it were, women wouldn't on average make 74 cents to every dollar a man makes. The measurement in a committed relationship is this and only this: Is each partner bringing everything he or she can to the relationship? That is the only measure that counts.

If we have a joint checking account, do we need individual checking accounts as well?
Individual accounts in addition to the joint account are, in my opinion, an absolute must. Grown-ups need discretionary income, after all. Sharing is very important in a committed relationship, but so is autonomy. Think about how you would feel if you had to ask for money for a new lipstick, or fishing tackle. You're partners, remember, and there are three entities here— yours, mine, and the big one, ours. Ours is most important, but yours and mine still count for a lot, too.

Net Worth and Self-worth

So you are saying that proportionally equal financial contributions give you equal power, and that equal power is important in a relationship?
That is exactly what I am saying. You need to discuss this right this minute with your partner, if you haven't already. Despite how you may feel some days, the truth is that the amount of money that you make when you are in a committed relationship does not make you more or less important or deserving or entitled to make decisions that affect both of you. Many people do incredibly meaningful work, *vital* work, yet are totally underpaid—teachers, social workers, stay-at-home moms—while others are paid exorbitant amounts for work that in the long run may not make a difference to one single soul. Do not—I repeat, do not—value yourself or your partner by how much money either of you makes. Enter the relationship, and continue in the relationship, as equals. Remember: People first, then money. If this is a problem for either of you, there is emotional work that you need to tackle now!

My partner and I have lived together for about three years, and I have supported her financially during that time. My income is quite high in comparison to hers, and it seems as if this discrepancy in incomes has created a huge chasm between us. She feels as if she will never be able to match my contributions to our relationship, so what's the point? How can I level the playing field without having to give up her or my income?

Different salary levels can be a real sticking point in a relationship, but they don't have to be. Money can be one of the most creative forces in the world, as well as one of the most destructive, but one thing I can say for sure is that money will always be a force that we have to deal with. Therefore, when someone has less money or simpler possessions than those around her—especially compared to the person with whom she is in a relationship—she's likely to feel there's a chasm between her and her partner. Finding a solution requires that you first acknowledge the problem, as you have done.

Then how do we bridge the gap created by our disparate incomes?

First of all, you should be extremely careful that you do not create an environment in which your partner feels that she is holding you back and keeping you from doing the kinds of things that you love, or that she is somehow less than a full person because she earns less money than you do. That's what can make her feel she will never have enough. Make sure you keep this in mind before you blurt out, "Hey, let's go to Paris for the weekend," or, "Let's go shopping at Tiffany, just for fun." Try eating at home, or else eat at places that she can afford to pay for as well, and talk with her about her perceptions of your different financial capacities. It is very important that you let her carry her own weight when it comes to money. Otherwise, before you know it she's going to feel powerless, which leads to feeling resentful.

In order for you to really bridge the gap, I want you to examine your own heart. Ask yourself honestly, do you feel your partner is worth less because she makes less? Ask yourself, is there anything that you can do to help her make more? Ask yourself, what is true equality and where does it lie? In your bank book? In your bedroom? In your heart?

If your partner asked me for advice, I would say this: Recognize that gifts of the heart are priceless. Your partner can buy virtually anything he wants for himself, but he can't buy love. Know that what you bring to this relationship has true, everlasting value that has nothing to do with money. You do, however, have to be strong and not overextend yourself financially just to keep up with him. You have to pay your own way when you can, and know when to draw the line when it comes to matching your partner's spending.

I make very little money, but my spouse or partner makes a lot—and says it's okay if I use my money for my own needs and don't contribute to the joint household bills. Will this work?
In my opinion, this won't work—in fact, chances are that as the years go by, it will backfire. When one person pays for everything, what usually ends up happening is that that person tends to feel a sense of ownership toward everything, as well as a creeping and unspoken resentment toward the person who is not paying his or her way. In a joint life, you *both* have to pay. What's more, the person who is not contributing financially ends up feeling less and less powerful, and feels he or she has less and less of a right to make joint financial decisions, which is both partners' right in a committed relationship. It is our nature to measure our self-worth in dollars and cents. When you are working for money but not contributing financially to your relationship, you will start to devalue yourself. It is far better to contribute on a fair percentage basis, even if just a few dollars a month, than to contribute nothing at all.

What if I would like to stop working for money and stay home to take care of the children?

The first thing you have to ask yourself is this: Is staying at home financially feasible? To answer this question, I recommend that you and your spouse add up all your expenses—everything from the mortgage to food to clothes and schooling for the children. How much is left over each month? If there's very little or nothing left over, and you both decide that this is the right course to follow anyway, then you must share equally in the responsibility of caring for and spending your money. If there is any discretionary money, it should be split fifty-fifty, regardless of who's bringing it in. Remember, in most states, all married couples' income is considered to be jointly owned, and that should be the guiding principle of your partnership.

If I do decide to stay home with the children, how do we live on one income?
There is no simple formula for "finding" the money in this situation. You and your spouse must work together to adjust the variables, whether it means seeking a higher-paying job for the partner who is earning money, moving to a more affordable house or apartment, or learning to make do without certain luxuries.

Once we've figured out the financial side of my staying home with the children, what else should my spouse and I think about?
After you've worked out your finances, the most important factor is that you and your spouse both agree that you will stay home with the children, because resentment on either side should tell you pretty clearly that the arrangement won't work. You must agree, too, that any assets that accumulate belong to both parties, not just to the partner earning money. And you must find a way to ensure that you both know that the partner staying home is a full, equal partner, with equal rights—

and isn't subtly belittled. After all, that person will be doing work equal to, if not more important than, that of someone who marches off to the office in a gray suit every morning.

The way we divide our expenses up, my husband made a monthly contribution to our joint checking account for the car payment. Now that the car is paid off, he said he shouldn't have to put that money into our joint checking account anymore.

You and your husband have a chance here to make some good money—so let's not blow it! When something gets paid off or a former expense (day care, for instance) disappears, the same amount of money should still be paid out at the same interval—into the investment vehicle you both choose—and go toward your future together.

Both my husband and I go to an office every day. What if—perish the thought—one of us loses our job?

If you lose your job through sickness or downsizing, through bad luck, or through no fault of your own, then your relationship must stretch to sustain you. If your relationship is good and strong (and elastic) enough, it can do this easily. Remember the extra 10 percent you were putting into your joint fund all along? Now you see why you put it there. That money is to help you both in times of trouble. This is true to the law and the spirit of marriage. And what is your role in all this? To get back on your feet as quickly as you can.

Once our individual and joint accounts are set up, how do we save for our future together?

The first way you should save for your future together is to contribute as much as you can to your employer's 401(k) or retirement plan and/or to an IRA. (If you are self-employed, fund a SEP-IRA or a KEOGH plan.) As your circumstances improve, you'll want to put money into a non–retirement-plan investment vehicles as well. Again, use a proportional-contribution approach to create money for your future, money that will be shared equally. If one of you makes a lot more money than the other and wants to invest more, it is up to both of you (or your pre-nup) to decide to whom that money will go in the event of a divorce.

PREVIOUS MARRIAGES

The man I'm about to marry has an ex-wife and two children whom he still supports. Will my income be considered by the court when it is deciding how much his alimony and child support payments will be?
Technically, no, it will not. However, the court will look at your joint household income and expenses. If your spouse has more disposable income because you and he have combined incomes, then your non-parental income has essentially entered the picture. Your income may be exempt from consideration if you and your husband keep your monies separate, although in some states the court can subpoena your income tax returns to find out your combined household income before setting (or changing) the amount of your husband's payments.

What are the presumptions of the court with respect to custody of children?
Courts in most states believe that joint legal custody is best for children and encourage joint physical custody as well. They will not award sole custody to a parent unless there's a strong

showing of proof of unfitness of the other parent. But courts in some states will not award joint custody unless both parties agree to it. Incidentally, this is one issue that can't be predisposed in a prenuptial agreement.

If my ex-spouse doesn't pay child support, can the court still enforce visitation rights?

Yes. Financial and custodial arrangements are considered by courts to be distinct and separate issues.

Who is responsible for an incapacitated child?

The father and mother share equal responsibility for an incapacitated or disabled child. In most states, when the child turns 18, he or she is considered a conserved adult (the age may vary from state to state); the parents become the conservators and manage any state or federal money for which the child is eligible. In turn, the state can access money that you or your spouse have put aside to be held for the benefit of the child. If you have a child (or, for that matter, a parent) who will need long-term assistance, please see a good trust lawyer who deals with asset protection.

AVOIDING DIVORCE

My wife and I are not getting along, and this has been the case for a long time. Before I look into divorce, what can we do to try to work things out?

There are many things you can do before you take that ultimate step. The first thing I would recommend is to look into the possibility of seeing a marriage counselor. I advise this because what usually happens when two people aren't getting along is that one or both of you retreat into silence and resentment. And if you do discuss the things that are bothering you, it is usually at earth-shattering volume—not calmly or rationally. Marriage counselors are trained therapists, usually psychologists or social workers, who will help you and your wife bring all the issues that are bothering you out into the open. They are impartial and trained not to take one side of an argument but to look at both sides and try to help work out compromises.

How do I choose a marriage counselor?

Look very carefully—your marriage is worth it. Make sure that the marriage counselor is a member of the American Association for Marriage and Family Therapy (AAMFT). Call the AAMFT for the names and phone numbers of qualified therapists in your area; call (202) 452-0109, or visit their website at *www.aamft.com.* If you don't like the first therapist you interview, then by all means interview another. If you can get a referral from a trusted friend, all the better. The important thing is that you and your spouse feel comfortable with the therapist, since some very intimate issues will be discussed in the office. If money is a problem for you, look in your phone book to see if there is a Family and Child Services, Inc., office near where you live. This is a nonprofit organization that offers counseling services on a sliding-fee scale.

What if my spouse refuses to go with me?

Go alone, then. A marriage involves two people, after all, and since you are one of them, you can at least help yourself. Even if your spouse doesn't want to go along, a good therapist will help you formulate and clarify the problems you are having with your relationship. But I would see a spouse's refusal to enter into marriage counseling as a pretty bad sign.

My husband and I tried marriage counseling, and it didn't work for us. We've reached an impasse. Any other ideas?

Sometimes taking a short vacation from each other can be a good idea. And I don't mean a vacation where you sit around in the sun drinking piña coladas, flirting with strangers. I recommend that you choose a time and a place when and where you can seriously think about the state of your marriage and whether or not divorce is the only option available to you. If you want to take a vacation with your spouse, spending some time alone together can work wonders for couples who are having troubles in their relationship or who feel estranged from each other.

SEPARATION

How is separation different from divorce?

Separation gives both partners the opportunity to find out what it would be like to live apart from each other—in separate residences and often with separate finances. In some states, you can apply for legal separation only as a prelude to divorce. In other states, you can be separated indefinitely, without ever getting a divorce. (Remember, though, in this case, you are still married.) Basically, separation is defined as no longer living together and no longer having the intention to reconcile. It is a kind of limbo, since one of you has probably moved out, but you are still married.

What is an informal separation?

If you are a couple who has agreed to separate informally, then all that means is that one of you has moved out. This usually happens in situations in which one or both of you feel as though you need time to think things over. While you may end up getting a divorce, this really isn't necessarily on either of your minds when you separate, whether for financial or religious reasons, or even for reasons having to do with the maintenance of your health insurance.

Then what is a legal separation?

In some states, moving out with no intention of returning constitutes a legal separation, which can fix the date for certain financial matters. Couples can also apply for a formal legal separation in cases when it is the first step toward filing for divorce. After filing a petition for separation with the county court, you can have your attorney prepare a legal separation, or else it can be an agreement that you and your spouse have drafted together.

Is one type of separation better than the other?

A lot depends on the intentions of the parties involved. A formal separation obviously spells out legal and financial matters much more clearly than an informal separation. A formal separation also guarantees greater certainty—for example, will your spouse support you financially during the period when you are living apart? What about custody arrangements if you have children together? How will you divide up the property that you share? This not only diminishes the possibility of strife and misunderstandings, but if you end up getting a divorce, then a lot of things will have already been set down on paper.

Is the date that you agree to separate important?

Yes. Depending on the state in which you live, the date of separation can matter a great deal in determining the financial outcome in a divorce and can affect, among other issues, how you'll divide retirement assets, how much alimony may be at stake, your right to a share of your spouse's Social Security payments, and your responsibility for any debt incurred by your spouse.

If you know or sense that you may be headed for divorce, try to plan your separation date with all these factors in mind. I learned firsthand how important setting the separation date can be when the husband of a very good friend of mine came home and announced, apparently out of the clear blue sky, that he wanted a divorce. He asked her to move out as soon as possible. I couldn't figure out what had happened and why it was all so sudden and urgent. A few days later, as my friend was preparing to move, I happened to read in the paper that the company her husband was working for had just been bought out and in two months all the employees were going to receive stock options as well as a generous pension plan. My friend's husband knew that if this took place after he and his wife were officially separated, there was a good chance that he wouldn't have to share that windfall with her. It was a tense two months, but she waited them out before she made her move.

Why do people separate in the first place? Shouldn't they just make up their minds to get a divorce or not get a divorce?
There are many different reasons why couples agree to separate. Some couples want to find out firsthand what living apart feels like. Other couples need to have time and space to analyze their relationships—what is right about them as well as what is wrong. If you are married to someone who has shown some kind of problematic behavior (for example, excessive drinking, cheating on you, or verbal or physical abuse), sepa-

rating shows that you are dead serious about wanting that person to change or else. Or you know that you want to get a divorce, and you can't bear the thought of living with your spouse until the divorce is official. Or you have religious or financial reasons for wanting to stay married a little longer. Finally, you may live in a state where you have to be legally separated before you can file for divorce.

Can I "date" my husband while the two of us are separated?

My advice would be to consult your attorney before you consider dating your spouse during a separation. A lot depends on whether or not you have filed (or are planning to file) for a divorce where one of you is at fault. Imagine if you filed for divorce from your husband on the grounds of mental cruelty. During your separation, you and he start dating again, to see if you can rekindle that spark that attracted you to each other in the first place. Well, it doesn't work out, and you go ahead with plans for the divorce on the basis of your spouse's mental cruelty. After it learns that you and your spouse were dating again, the court is probably not going to take your complaint very seriously!

But what if my spouse and I intend to reconcile somewhere along the line?

Again, I would consult your attorney. But in general, if you and your spouse are planning to reconcile, I don't see a problem in your sharing a few pizzas.

What are the downsides of separating from my spouse?

In many cases, the downsides are financial, since you may have come to rely on your spouse's income, and without it your expenses will seem to mount. In the worst-case scenario, you may not have enough money to rent or buy a new place and support yourself, and you may be cut off from the prospective income of your spouse. Emotionally speaking, you may just be putting off the inevitable—i.e., divorce—and simply postponing the fact of the matter, which is that it is now time for you to start getting on with your new life, alone. And remember, even though you are living apart, you and your spouse are still married and still responsible for each other's debts.

How do things stand legally if I tell my spouse I want to separate? And what if I move out?
It depends on what state you live in. In some states, if you want to separate but your husband doesn't, you may have just unwittingly given him grounds for a fault divorce. Also, in some states, you can be charged with desertion if you separate informally. This won't look very good if and when you decide to file for divorce.

Is there any way I can protect myself legally?
Yes. Make sure that all these issues are covered and very carefully worded in the separation agreement that you work out with your spouse and each of your attorneys.

My husband and I have just agreed to a separation. Where should I concentrate my efforts, money-wise?
Once a separation seems inevitable, you must turn your attention to money issues as quickly as possible. If you procrastinate, you may one day find that you are responsible for credit card debt that was incurred after you moved out, or that one of your joint accounts has been wiped clean of all its assets, or that the home equity account that was there in case of emergencies now has a loan against it for $20,000, for which you are responsible. Do not be afraid to separate your

accounts immediately—this is looking after your best interests, after all. And remember, if you should end up getting back together, you can always open those accounts again.

In specific financial terms, what exactly should I do?
What follows is an overview of everything that should be done immediately when it becomes clear that a separation is imminent:

- Consult with an attorney regarding the divorce laws in your particular state, and their applicability to your particular situation.
- If you don't already have one, open up an account in your name only.
- Close all joint accounts. Don't freeze accounts, because one or both of you may need access to the funds for any number of reasons. With your attorneys' approval, split the money from joint accounts equally.
- Make copies of all the financial documents that show your true debts, assets, and expenses, including household and credit card bills, bank records, and expenses for the children—every penny you spend to live month to month.
- Start keeping track of all debts incurred and money paid to each other after the date of separation. This includes money spent on joint bills, improvements to the home, moving expenses, children, insurance premiums—everything that could pertain to the two of you. If you decide to pay support to your spouse while you are working things out, make sure that all these sums are documented, and that you have an agreement in writing as to what these funds are for. If you put this in writing, these payments may be tax-deductible, al-

though they will be considered taxable income to your spouse.

• See a tax specialist to decide whether you are going to file your taxes jointly or separately.

• Sit down and really figure out what you are worth as a couple. First determine the worth of everything you own jointly. It is essential, too, that you work with a tax specialist who can inform you of the tax consequences of every move you make.

• Gather documentation of all your assets—any investments, retirement plans, bonds, mutual funds, savings or money market accounts, etc. In addition, a tricky and relatively new area is that of stock options, which are given to employees at great discounts, but may not be exercised until years later. If your spouse has any stock options, you must see an attorney at once, as most states are still sorting out whether, in a divorce, a stock option that you hold today should be considered a joint asset when it is able to be exercised, however many years down the road.

• After you determine what you have in assets, as well as your expenses and income, try to sit down with your spouse and see if you can work out an equitable arrangement. Don't do this before you have all your documentation, however, because you can't negotiate without the facts, and don't agree to anything without consulting an attorney.

• Reduce your spending wherever possible to generate some savings for the rocky road ahead.

What about debt? Once we are separated, am I still responsible for any and all debts that my spouse has incurred during our marriage?

In most scenarios, the date of separation in a final judgment or decree officially determines when you are no longer responsible for the debts that your spouse incurs. Make sure all joint accounts are closed and divided when you separate. Make sure, too, that you divide all debts and know who is responsible for each one. Before doing so, set up an account in your name and make sure that you qualify for credit, since sometimes your individual credit rating can be affected if you close out an account. Contact all professionals and service providers (doctors, lawyers, dentists, etc.) and inform them in writing that if any work is being done for your spouse, you will not be responsible for the bills. The IRS has recently loosened its rules regarding "innocent spouses," making it easier to disavow the debts of an ex-spouse, so be sure to check with your accountant about any potential tax liabilities. Even if all these precautions are taken, it's still possible that creditors might come after you seeking payment for bills your spouse incurred. Thus the more accounts you can close, the better off you are. Note, too, that most likely you will be responsible for debts your spouse runs up for the necessities of life during the separation period. Necessities of life include housing, food, clothes, children's expenses, and medical expenses.

Please note that the hardest part of separation and/or divorce, for many people, is money. People can move away from each other and start new lives, either temporarily or forever, but often they seem unable to cut the financial ties quite as cleanly. Sometimes letting go of jointly managed money seems like the ultimate move, and they're not ready to do that yet. For other couples, simply living in two places increases their costs of living, and may force them to sell their house. In other cases, guilt keeps the money together. Or the person who has always handled the money keeps handling it because it's familiar and easy, or because both parties are simply too lazy to separate the funds. But whatever the reason, it is wrong to remain financially intimate after you have severed domestic and emotional ties.

Why is financial intimacy bad if my spouse and I are separated?

I have seen it time and time again: When someone continues to foot the bills after a separation, resentment builds up on one side, and on the other, there is an unhealthy dependence. At issue may be the house payment, let's say, until one spouse can find him- or herself a new place to live, or a car payment. Whatever the case, power and respect are going out the window on both ends. A brief deferral to avoid having to sell your house suddenly and ill-advisedly is certainly worth considering, but don't wait too long to separate your financial lives.

If you decide to pay for items for your spouse after you have separated, it is very important to set a start and a stop date. Set a time limit. The particulars of any financial arrangement between the two of you should be put in writing so that there is no misunderstanding. Remember, when one person is in shock—usually the person who is being left—he or she is not going to hear things accurately or remember things clearly. Do not set yourselves up for additional misunderstandings. With your attorneys' help, put your temporary agreement in writing, and both of you sign it and keep a copy.

THE EMOTIONS OF DIVORCE

To my great disappointment, my marriage hasn't worked out, and my husband and I have decided to split up. I never thought this would happen, and I al-

ternate between panic and fear. What should I be think-
ing about?

Believe it or not, you will get through this, just as you have gotten through other difficult times in your life. How you get through this, however, will largely be determined by whether you reach for your courage or turn away from it toward your feelings of pain and helplessness. During this transition period, you are going to have to make quite a few decisions, and it is vital that when you do so, your mind and body are as strong as possible. Act with strength, which itself will create strength. Eat well, exercise, allow yourself plenty of sleep. Even if the motions feel hollow at first, the actions are powerful, and powerful actions will nourish your courage.

It is also very important for you to remember that when you got married, you and your mate gave your word that you would honor each other for better or for worse, forever. Now that you are facing a divorce, you are breaking your vow in the practical realm, but you must still honor the "for worse" part of that promise on the emotional level—if only for your own sake. Your thoughts, your words, and every single action you take at this time will govern your way into the future and give you control over it.

How can my thoughts and words give me control over my future?

I'm a firm believer in the notion that your thoughts and your words create your destiny. One of my favorite books is a 10th-century Hindu text called *The Outlook of Shiva,* written by a scholar named Somananda. In it, Somananda instructs us to act as if we already embody our goal, no matter the disparity between what we are and how we feel now, and what we wish to become or achieve. It is important for us not to allow doubt or sadness or anger or confusion to cause us to abandon our intention. Instead, we must begin by clarifying our highest and noblest goals, and then we should try to maintain "an unwavering awareness" by affirming these goals with confidence and conviction. In this way, Somananda explains, our being aligns itself with our intention, and our goal becomes manifest. In short, become it by thinking it. Be it by saying it.

What do my thoughts and words have to do with how I'm feeling as I face the end of my marriage?
More than you might think. If your thoughts and words are full of hate, anger, and rage, then those emotions will direct your actions, and your actions will be actions of poverty. No matter how sad and angry and full of hate you may feel right now—and by the way, sadness and anger and hatred may be perfectly appropriate emotions for you to be feeling, depending on your situation—I ask you to recognize these feelings and how they can get in the way of your judgment, erase all the good in your past, and set the tone of your future. If instead you can carefully and deliberately draw upon your courage, faith, and grace during this hard time, you will be drawing on qualities of richness and taking those qualities with you into tomorrow. Whether you are the one who is being left or the one who is leaving, the way in which you behave during this period will live on with you, long after the pain of the divorce has faded. It will shape the life you lead after your marriage has ended.

Sometimes I feel as if going through the death of somebody I love would be less difficult than a divorce.
You're not alone. Over the years, I have come to believe that a death—whether foreseeable or unexpected—is in some ways easier to cope with, over the long term, than a divorce. Why?

Because with death there usually is no blame. With a death, everybody suffers loss—the person who's died and the loved ones left behind. A life is gone. The community gathers around you in mourning. Friends and relatives, some of whom you may not have seen in years, check in often to see how you are doing. If you have children, they draw closer to you. There is usually not much ambiguity, emotional or financial. The house is yours to sell or keep as you see fit, the car is yours, the retirement account, the life insurance policy, the possessions— everything that was "ours" is now yours. When you lose someone you love, the loss is enormous, to be sure. But you don't lose the love, which remains pure.

So in emotional as well as financial terms, divorce is actually very different from experiencing the death of a loved one?
Yes. If you are the bereaved party in the event of a divorce, you may be faced with an ex-partner who is living a perfectly happy life, perhaps with somebody else. You may feel that for all you gave to the relationship, you got little back in return. You may also be filled with regrets about how you behaved, fearing that maybe you forced your partner to leave you. Perhaps you are making do with less while your former partner is living on more. If you have children, your former partner may take them away from you one or two nights a week and every other weekend and show them a great time. The children themselves are likely to be as confused and angry as you are. As for the community, not everyone is rallying around you unconditionally, the way they probably would have if your spouse had died; no one's dropping off supper for you, and the phone is hardly ringing off the hook. Instead, some of your friends may feel uncomfortable around you. In fact, some of

them may be taking your ex-spouse's side, thus compounding your loss. To rebuild your life from this point of disequilibrium will take enormous courage.

I am so full of hatred toward the person who came between my husband and me that I don't know what to do!
Of course you feel this way, especially if you're being left for someone else—even if you recognize that the person who comes between people rarely comes uninvited. Nevertheless, if all your energies are devoted to hate or revenge, you won't have a whole lot left for more constructive pursuits. If you think about this hate all the time, then you'll talk about it, and act on it, and you will be building a hateful, vengeful foundation on which to live the rest of your life. Try to pull away from the hate as much as you can and instead expend your energies on caring for yourself.

Where should I even begin to cope with the emotions of separation and divorce?
As I said, a good place to start is by remembering that every action you take today will have an effect tomorrow. Are you saying to yourself, "I've never been so angry in my life"? If you are, you should keep in mind that acting from anger not only threatens to impair your good judgment when it comes to making vital decisions, it can also increase your attorney's fees.

How can my anger cost me more money?
When I've worked with clients who are going through divorces, I have noticed a direct correlation between the amount of the bills and the amount of anger the person has. What usually happens to people who angrily refuse to settle with their partners? They end up spending a lot more time in conflict—and paying a lot more money as a result.

So anger has a financial as well as an emotional cost. Just how much more does it cost to not settle or compromise?

On average, an in-court divorce trial can cost as much as three times as much as an out-of-court settlement, for two reasons. First, those who go to court usually haven't a clue as to how their case will end up, because through the lens of their self-righteousness and anger, they see only one side—theirs. And if the court's decision is at odds with their expectations, they get angrier still. Even if they "win," there is no guarantee whatsoever that their anger will subside, for what often happens is that a disgruntled ex-spouse may refuse to comply with the court order, and then the anger escalates to a whole new level. Better to have been aware of your anger in the first place and to have done something about it. And second, even if you "win" at trial, you may have spent more than the amount of your settlement on lawyer's fees to arrive at this "victory."

Are you saying that I shouldn't take my divorce to trial even if my ex-spouse is being completely unreasonable?

No. If your estranged spouse is being unreasonable and there seems to be no amicable way to resolve your differences, do not be afraid to go to court to have the judge determine the final accounting, assign responsibility for any debts, divide any remaining assets, and settle issues of child and spousal support, attorneys' fees, and so on. Sometimes it is better to have a rational judge decide your fate rather than let your angry spouse (or your angry self!) call the shots. You must do this, however, with eyes that are clear, and unhampered by any toxic emotions that can prevent you from seeing the truth.

In addition to anger, what are some other reactions people have when they are facing a divorce?

A common reaction of my clients is to insist they don't care about the outcome of the divorce, or about what happens to their ex-spouse or to themselves. "I just want to get all this behind me and get on with my life," they say. There are other destructive phrases, too, that I hear a lot. "I'm going to take him to the cleaners." Or "I don't want anything. He [or she] can have it all." Or "I'm not worried about the money. I know he [or she] will be fair." None of these is a worthwhile attitude or belief. Revenge will get you nowhere, fast. The martyr approach, letting your spouse have everything, makes no sense, either emotionally or financially. You were half of this marriage, after all. As for believing that your estranged spouse will be fair to you, since he has been fair to you up to this point, well, when it comes to dividing assets—which means giving up money—people can behave very strangely, and someone you once thought of as the most generous person in the world might turn overnight into someone entirely different.

If you find yourself thinking or saying any of these phrases, I want to ask you: Are you still being mindful of the awesome power of words? Do you remember that when you say you don't care what happens, you are in effect creating a situation that almost surely will prevent you from getting on with your life in a rich and productive way? Remember, you may spend many more years divorced from your spouse than you spent married to him, or her; therefore, the decisions you make during this crucial time will affect you for many years to come. Do not take casually what is happening to you right now. Divorce is as serious a commitment to the future as marriage was. Now is the time I need you to summon words of wealth.

What do you mean by words of wealth?

Words of wealth are words like these: "I want to get on with my life, but I care deeply about what happens now, because

what happens now will affect me and possibly my children forever." You must be mindful of the present tense, and also keep
in mind how swiftly the future becomes the present. And the
future may not involve just you, but your children, and their
children. Say the words of wealth to your attorney and to your
ex, and say them with grace until they become true.

*I don't really care about the money—I just want my
wife back!*
So often when divorce is imminent, the person who is being
left finds it very hard to face up to what is happening. He or
she starts thinking or saying things like, "I can get her back if
I do whatever she wants." But when you give up your rights to
money and make it seem totally unimportant, you are not one
iota likelier to save your marriage. All you are likely to do with
this kind of thinking is impoverish your future, financially *and*
emotionally. With thoughts and words like the ones above,
you are about to serve yourself a double whammy. Not only
will you repel money, money that is rightfully yours, but the
person you are trying to bring closer will be repelled, too—by
your lack of self-respect and your powerlessness. No one is attracted to weakness. Maybe you can put your marriage back
together, maybe not. But please don't base your financial actions (or, for that matter, your emotional actions) on a tenuous
possibility. Protective action on your part will have absolutely
no effect on a possible reconciliation, I can promise you that.
If anything, your actions now—strong, powerful, clear, grace-
ful, and yes, rich—will better the chances for a reconciliation.

*And in the meantime, you're telling me to be very watch-
ful of my feelings, day in and day out.*
Yes. Count on feeling great one day, and the next day feeling
wretched. On the days that the blues hit you big time, give

yourself permission to take a break. Try not to make any decisions on those days if you don't have to. For the first six months after your breakup, rate yourself on a scale of one to ten twice a day—when you get up and about eight hours later—a one rating being extremely happy and ten being miserable. If ever you feel you are a five or more, then please do not make any decisions regarding your money or your divorce on that day. If you are asked to, simply say, "Not today, thank you," let it go at that, and address the matter when you feel better. Remember, check yourself *twice* a day, because sometimes a phone call, a song on the radio, a comment from a friend, or even two people walking down the street holding hands can set off a chain of emotions changing a one to an eight before you know what hit you. "Not today, thank you," is an expression of self-respect, coming from a position of power.

I am the person who was left. What angers me the most is that my ex-husband seems to be doing so much better than I am. How can I get myself to start doing as well as he seems to be?

Please realize that you are not in a contest to see who can get through this divorce with the fewest breakdowns or, for that matter, the fewest emotions. If you are the one who was left, do not be surprised if your spouse seems to be doing much better than you are. Try to be glad your spouse is thriving, as this will certainly make your life easier! Remember that the chances are pretty good that he or she has been thinking about this divorce for a long time, long enough to get used to the idea, whereas for you, it is brand-new and devastating. Your job now is to rebuild your life by identifying and then acting in your own best interests. Do not get pushed into doing anything during this difficult time. Start doing your daily ratings immediately and take action only when you feel ready. You have the power to set the pace of the divorce. You have the power, too, to drag it out, but that won't help you. Use your power wisely, to proceed as you are ready to.

I urge you to seek therapy or counseling if you can possibly afford it and/or to consult a member of the clergy. There is nothing wrong with receiving sympathy and emotional support from family and friends. But if you constantly allow them to see you at your very lowest point, it will be harder for you to restore the equilibrium of your relationships later, when you feel stronger. You don't want them to treat you like a victim for the rest of your life, do you? Plus, what if you need more than sympathy? A professional counselor's impartiality may help make you stronger, both in the short and long term. (Take care choosing one: As in every profession, there are good practitioners, and less good ones.) If there are children involved, a counselor may also help you in dealing with their pain and confusion and deciding whether they, too, need professional help.

I left my wife and now I am overcome by all sorts of emotions that I find it hard to live with. Any advice?
As the person who left, your responsibilities are immense. Regardless of your feelings today, you have just delivered a terrible blow to the person who was once the love of your life. For your own benefit, as well as your ex-spouse's, I want you to proceed slowly and with compassion. Your marriage didn't work out. Now it is your responsibility to conclude it as successfully as possible. How you end something as profound and important as a marriage is a reflection of how you live your life—financially, emotionally, and spiritually.

ANNULMENTS

I am a practicing Roman Catholic, and I am wondering if instead of a separation and a divorce I can get my five-year marriage annulled.

There are two different kinds of annulments, a legal annulment and a religious annulment. The latter is associated with the Catholic Church. If you are Catholic and you divorce and wish to marry someone else, the church will not formally recognize your new marriage until your old marriage is annulled.

How do I go about getting a religious annulment?

If you are a divorced Roman Catholic and you want to remarry under the auspices of that church, you should first make an appointment to see your parish priest. Next, a church court, known as a marriage tribunal, meets to discuss all the elements of your previous marriage, including the reasons leading to the divorce. During this meeting, the tribunal may ask you to provide a list of friends and family who were "witnesses" to your marriage, as well as certain legal documents pertaining to your marriage, such as your marriage license.

Will the church contact my ex-husband?

Yes, it will. He will be notified by the marriage tribunal that you want your marriage to be annulled. He then has the right to show the tribunal proof that your marriage was valid. Next the tribunal will review all the evidence, written and oral, and decide whether or not, according to the policies of the

Catholic Church, you have grounds for an annulment. If they say no, you have the right to appeal. If you lose your appeal, you can take your request for annulment all the way to Rome!

How long does a church annulment take?
Anywhere from several months to several years.

You mentioned a legal annulment. How does this work?
A legal annulment is a court order that basically announces to the world that your marriage was never legally valid to begin with—it's as though your marriage never took place.

But my marriage did take place! Why would a court declare it invalid?
The most common reason that a court is willing to declare an annulment is that one spouse lied to, or misled, the other. The assumption is that if the spouse who was lied to had known the truth, he or she would not have gotten married. Other reasons include a bigamous marriage (one in which your partner was already married), a marriage in which one of the parties wasn't of legal age, a marriage in which one of you was forced into wedlock, or a marriage that took place while one or both of you was intoxicated or under the influence of drugs.

Are legal annulments available in all states, or just a few?
Legal annulments are available in most states. Remember, though, that if you and your partner have children, an annulment will not have any effect—nor should it—on your responsibilities as a parent.

DIVORCE

Why are so many people getting divorced these days? It wasn't always that way, was it?

No, it wasn't. For whatever reason—changing times, sexual and women's liberation, or a generation that has different expectations of what a marriage should be and is less willing to "stick it out"—the fact of the matter is that these days, one in two marriages ends up in divorce. Of the 50 states, Nevada ranks first with the highest divorce rate, with Massachusetts bringing up the bottom.

How much does it cost to get a divorce?

That depends on a lot of different factors, the most important being whether your divorce is amicable, or whether you and your spouse are willing to fight it out to the bitter end. You can get divorced for a few hundred dollars, or you can spend a few thousand dollars, or you can go all out and spend a small fortune litigating a long divorce trial in court. But no matter what state you live in, it is a pretty good rule of thumb that the more issues you and your spouse can agree on, the less you will have to spend on attorneys' fees. Also, obviously, the more experienced or well-known the attorney you retain, the greater his or her fees will be.

Can I get an estimate of how much things will cost from several different attorneys?

Yes. Many divorce lawyers offer free 15- to 20-minute consultations. Request estimates based on several possible divorce scenarios. These will only be approximations, of course, but they will still give you a pretty good idea of how much things will cost you in the end. Interviewing a cross-section of lawyers is a good idea for another reason, too: One attorney may tell you that the things you want out of your divorce are impossible to get; another attorney may promise you the moon but in the end disappoint you. Consulting with several attorneys can help give you a good fix on what is possible and what is not.

So how do I find a really great divorce attorney?

Don't just let your fingers do the walking through the Yellow Pages here. Get a referral from friends who have been in the same boat. A shrewd, experienced attorney is essential, particularly if your divorce proceedings promise to be bitter or drawn out. If this is the case, you should try to find someone who has had extensive courtroom experience. You also should be conscious of whether you want a conciliator or a gladiator. In general, you should make it a priority to find an attorney who is experienced in family law. He or she should be someone that you feel very comfortable with, though it is also important to remember here that your attorney is not your best friend or your confidant, but your lawyer and your advocate.

Are there any resources other than referrals for finding a good divorce lawyer?

Yes. Go to your public library and see if they have a copy of the Martindale-Hubbell directory, which lists and evaluates lawyers state by state, city by city. Or call the American Academy of Matrimonial Lawyers or go to their website at *www.aaml.org.*

I am about to meet with my divorce attorney. What should I bring with me?

One of the very first things, if not *the* first thing, you should do when you are preparing for a divorce, is to make a complete list of what you own, and what your spouse owns—basically, a list of all your assets. By assets, I mean the value of your various bank accounts, CDs, any retirement or profit-sharing plans you hold individually or in common, money market funds, stocks, bonds, mutual funds, real estate, jewelry, art, houses, furnishings, and automobiles. You should also create an inventory of your outstanding debt, whether it's credit card debt, a mortgage, or a student loan. And if you are looking for spousal or child support, you need to know what your monthly budget typically is.

DIVIDING ASSETS IN DIVORCE

I dread dividing up the assets from our 14-year marriage. How do courts and attorneys go about deciding who gets what?

Let me start by saying that in the suite next to my office is an attorney who deals with family issues and divorce, and her rule-of-thumb advice is to choose your battles carefully. If there is a lot of property to be divided, my advice is to concede gracefully on the smaller stuff and you'll be on higher ground when it comes to the items that really matter. In short, it's not worth fighting over who gets the orange towels.

In general, the court system is in place to see to the division of property and debts and to settle issues of spousal support, child support, custody, and visitation. In some states, everything is divided fifty-fifty, but in other states, the judge has wide discretion to divide assets and debts and to fix spousal support based on equitable principles of need.

What are some of the points that the court considers when dividing assets?

The court most commonly considers the following issues: the duration of the marriage; the earning power of each party, i.e., how well each of you is equipped to maintain your present standard of living; the marketable skills of the party seeking support; how long the party who has been supported until now has stayed at home; whether children will make it harder for the party seeking support to find work; and what would be involved, i.e., time and expenses, to educate or retrain the stay-at-home partner for the current job market. The court's goal is that the party seeking support will eventually be able to support him- or herself. The trend in many states is to award support for a period of time equal in length to half the duration of the marriage, without regard to fault. The court also considers the means of the partner who is being asked for support, and child support and custody arrangements, when applicable. In determining child support, the court often looks to the percentage of time the child or children spend with each parent and the respective incomes of each parent. The court will also consider, age, health, and extenuating circumstances, such as whether you're caring for an invalid child or parent.

How do I determine the value of my car? It's five years old!

It's not as hard as you might think. Ask several local car dealers what they would give you for your vehicle. (Take into consideration the fact that dealers tend to quote you a low price.) Another good bet is to check your car's so-called "Blue Book" value. The Blue Book, also known as the *Official Used Car Guide* and published by the National Association of Used Car Dealers, lists the adjusted prices of all used cars. If you can't find it in your local library, go to the association's website at *www.kbb.com.*

My spouse and I have lived in the same house for 12 years. Now that we're getting divorced, how will the court decide who gets to stay and who has to go?
The hardest decision most divorcing couples face is who gets to keep or stay in the home that the two of you built. It is hard to give up not only a person but also the space that you felt safe—and probably happy—in for a long time. Who keeps the house and who moves out can be a murky legal area, because the law does not mandate who must move out.

What if there are children involved?
When there are children involved, it's another story. The primary caretaker usually is allowed to stay in the house with the children until the children reach 18 years of age. If you are the primary caretaker, please see an attorney before you do anything, because if you moved out and there's a subsequent legal battle for the house, many judges will lean toward keeping the situation as it is rather than disrupting the children's lives yet again. If there is any physical threat to the children, then you must seek a restraining order that would prevent your spouse from staying in the house. Usually though, the decision will be made between the two of you, alone or with the aid of legal counsel or a mediator (more about them later).

My husband and I have agreed to sell our house rather than haggle over it. How do we figure out how much it is worth?
Many people decide to go this route. Again, you should use local resources. Contact a real estate agent and see if he or she can provide some recent selling prices of houses comparable to

yours in your neighborhood. If you don't feel satisfied with the answers you get, it might be worth your while to hire a real estate appraiser. The important thing to remember is not to value your house based on its tax appraisal, since tax appraisals are typically considerably less than what your house is actually worth.

What are the capital gains rules these days about selling a house?

In 1997, Congress changed the rules regarding capital gains on the sale of your primary residence—and they changed it in the taxpayer's favor. If you are single, you get a capital gains exclusion of $250,000. This means you won't be taxed on the first $250,000 of profit from the sale of your house. Married couples receive an exclusion of $500,000. The only glitch is that you have to have lived in your house for at least two of the five years prior to your selling it to be eligible for the exclusion. Keep this time limit in mind if you are thinking of moving out but deferring the sale of the house for a few years.

Is this a one-time-only exclusion?

More good news from Congress—no. You can use this exclusion every two years, as many times as you want.

Do I have to "roll over" the proceeds of my sale into a new property?

No. The so-called "rollover" provision, which allowed you to benefit from this capital gains exclusion only if you agreed to buy a new house of equal or greater value to the one you just sold, is now a thing of the past.

What happens if my husband and I make more than $500,000 from the sale of our house?

Then whatever amount in excess of the $500,000 exclusion will be taxed at around 20 percent, and somewhere between 10 percent and 15 percent for people in lower tax brackets. There's hope for the future, however. Congress has announced that in 2001, this tax rate will be reduced to 18 percent, and for those people in lower tax brackets, to 8 percent.

Can I throw my spouse out of the house, especially if I owned the house before we got married?

It is a staple of state law that "neither spouse may be excluded from the other's dwelling." If a domestic situation becomes violent, barring the violent partner from the house requires a court-issued restraining order.

How do you divide up the value of your house?

The value of the house is set on the date of divorce, not the separation date. In other words, let's say you decide that the marriage is over, and you and your spouse separate and you move out. Two years later, the divorce is final. If the value of the house has increased over those two years, you will get to participate in that increase in value.

If you are unmarried, the house issues will be resolved according to the property laws of your state. In most states, this means that neither one of you has the right to buy out the other one; if you can't make a deal amicably, the court will sell the house and divide the proceeds. These are usually divided equally unless one of the partners can prove an agreement to the contrary. For these reasons, working out an amicable settlement in which one party buys out the other or they sell the place jointly is always the best solution.

Can your spouse leave you, move to another state, and sue for divorce there to get a better deal for him- or herself?

Yes. This is why many high-profile figures who divorce try to get the proceedings switched to a community-property state, where the split is fifty-fifty. Bear in mind, though, that divorce laws vary widely from state to state, particularly those regarding residency requirements before filing for and being granted a divorce.

If I move from one state to another, can my marital property rights change?

Yes, and sometimes drastically. For example, if you move to California and you own property in another state that you acquired during the marriage, it may be considered quasi-community property. Accordingly, you may have to split it in the event of a divorce. Quasi-community property is an asset that would be considered community property if it was acquired or located in the state you are in when you divorce, but may not be considered as such in the state where it is located.

In a divorce, can a spouse take back a gift given specifically to you—or at least claim his or her "half" of such a gift?

Not if it really was a gift. But transfers often can be ambiguous, and thus, the gift-giver may be able to claim that whatever changed hands wasn't really a gift after all.

I suspect my soon-to-be ex-spouse is hiding assets. Is there anything I can do to force him to disclose everything he owns?

In many states there are particular requirements of disclosure for a divorce. If you later discover that there were hidden assets, the court can award all of them to you—not just the 50 percent you might otherwise have been granted. You can always reopen your divorce action if you believe your ex-spouse defrauded you in the settlement. This holds true in every state.

DIVORCE AND RETIREMENT BENEFITS

My spouse and I each count our retirement plans among our assets. At what point does the court begin to assess the value of our retirement plans?

Many states value retirement plans and/or benefits from the date of separation, not from the date of divorce, because this date marks the point at which a couple's common interest ended. Keep this in mind, because it may affect what you or your spouse is entitled to. For instance, many employers make their contributions to their employees' pension plans at the end of the calendar year. If you separated from your spouse and moved out on December 24, and on December 25 the employer made the annual pension contribution, you may very well have missed out on your right to claim any portion of that year's contribution. (Many self-employed people, on the other hand, put the year's retirement money into their KEOGHs or SEP-IRAs at the very last minute of the tax year, in April, and this should be considered as well.)

Make sure, then, you know how your and/or your spouse's pension plan works. When are the valuations of it made? If a pension plan is involved, consult an attorney before making any move and obtain a copy of the benefit schedule for both your and your spouse's retirement plan.

What about Social Security? Am I entitled to any of my spouse's benefits when we get divorced?

Again, let me start with a recent memory. Another client of mine decided that she wanted to divorce her husband, and she wanted to do it immediately. Luckily, it promised to be a very amicable divorce. They had seen an attorney and had papers drawn up, which she was about to sign when she called to ask me a question about their investments. They had both been clients of mine for a long time, and I wondered how long they had been married. When I asked her, she told me nearly 10 years. I suggested she wait, because if she went ahead and signed those papers right away, she would not, when the time came, be entitled to Social Security benefits based on her spouse's earnings. Social Security benefits are based on the date of divorce, not the date of separation. Since my client had never worked outside the home and hadn't built up Social Security of her own, signing the divorce papers before their 10th anniversary would have turned out to be a big mistake. If she wanted to, I told her, she could move out, they could separate, and for all intents and purposes go on with their lives as if they were divorced. Then, after their 10th anniversary, they could sign all the necessary papers to make it legal.

Waiting to pass the 10-year mark affected not only my client's Social Security but also her alimony. The seven-to-ten-year mark is important because many states use these anniversaries as benchmarks for what constitutes a long-term marriage. A long-term marriage judgment may play very favorably for purposes of spousal support for a spouse who has not worked outside the home or who was earning very little during the marriage.

What criteria do I have to meet in order to be eligible for my former husband's Social Security benefits?
Curiously enough, this is a matter that you have to work out between the Social Security Administration and you, not between you and your former spouse. You may very well be entitled to retirement benefits if you are at least 62 years old; you are not married when you apply for benefits; you are not al-

ready receiving Social Security spousal or survivor benefits; and you and your ex-spouse were married for at least ten years, and you and he have been divorced for two years.

How do I establish my eligibility for Social Security benefits?

You should visit the Social Security office nearest where you live at least three months before you turn 62. You should bring along with you proof of your identity, your age (as well as of the age of your former spouse), your marriage, and your divorce.

But I feel guilty about claiming part of my ex-husband's Social Security benefits!

Claiming your share of your former spouse's Social Security benefits is a right you are entitled to by the federal government and does not diminish your spouse's Social Security check in the least. So don't fail to claim your due because you think you will be taking something away from your spouse, because that is absolutely not the case.

DIVORCE FACTS

My husband and I have been separated for a year. I've retained an attorney and have made a list of all my assets and liabilities. How do I go about filing for divorce?

During the separation, one of you will file a petition for divorce or a complaint in the appropriate court in your or your spouse's county of residence (the name of the court varies from state to state), and this will start the formal divorce proceedings. If you do the filing, you are considered the plaintiff, or the petitioner. Your spouse is considered the defendant, or the respondent.

What goes into a petition for divorce?

Your petition simply puts forth the facts of where and when you were married, when you separated, your key financial assets, and the number of children who will be affected by the divorce. It also indicates what you want from your spouse, whether it's spousal support, child support, custody of the children, etc.

Does my spouse get a copy of this petition?

After you file your petition, your spouse must be notified and acknowledge formally that you have filed. He may sign what is called a waiver of service, which basically means that he will not be served formally by a process server. This usually happens if a couple has agreed to divorce amicably. If the opposite is true, then your spouse will be served by a process server.

What if for some reason my spouse can't be served—if I don't know where he is, for example? Does this mean we have to stay married forever?

Don't worry, the answer is no. In most states, you can publish a legal notice in your local paper informing your spouse that you have filed a petition for divorce.

We have two children together. What about them?

If there are children involved, this is the time when one of you may need to file a request for temporary child and spousal support, and for custody, visitation rights, alimony—or anything else that may apply to your situation—with the local court handling your divorce. You will receive from the court a temporary order soon after this filing, and a permanent order once the divorce is final. Even after that, the court has the right to alter child support provisions until the children are emancipated, i.e., until they turn 18; thus both ex-spouses can petition the court for a change in support payments or custody arrangements until their children become legal adults. The court also retains jurisdiction over spousal support until that is terminated.

Can child support obligations stop before my child turns 18?

Yes, if your child goes into the military; if he or she takes on a full-time permanent job; if he or she gets married; or if he or she dies.

I am paying my wife child support for our three children. Are these payments considered tax-deductible by the IRS?

No. Relatedly, if you are a child receiving child support, it is not considered taxable income by the IRS.

What comes after the temporary order?

Next comes the process known as legal discovery—informal or formal—which determines exactly what assets must be divided. If you have children, this information is used to calculate the amount of child support or alimony that you will have to pay, or that you will receive.

How long does the discovery process take?

It can take anywhere from a week or two up to several months, depending on whether or not you and your spouse agree on things.

What's the difference between informal and formal discovery?

Informal discovery is when your attorney asks your spouse's attorney for information, whether financial, legal, or medical, and your spouse is willing to answer each question honestly and to the best of his ability. Basically, he voluntarily discloses the information that your attorney requires. Formal discovery becomes necessary if your spouse will not provide information needed by your attorney and involves subpoenas for documents and depositions under oath.

My attorney told me that I am going to be deposed. What should I keep in mind during the deposition process?

A deposition can be nerve-wracking, so try to keep calm. Answer all questions truthfully, no matter how painful it may be, but at the same time, be very careful about what you say. Try to keep your answers brief and factual, and do not stray from the question that's being asked. If you give more information than what was asked for, you may inadvertently harm your case.

What if my spouse refuses to be deposed?

You can request a court order requiring him to appear at a deposition. If your spouse violates the court order, he will risk being held in contempt of court, which might lead to the judge's immediately ruling in your favor.

COLLABORATIVE LAW

I have heard the term "collaborative law." What does it mean?

Collaborative law is a fairly new option for working out all the issues involved in your divorce. It involves you, your spouse, and your attorneys sitting down together to figure out a divorce settlement that is fair to you and your spouse. (The attorneys must have training in the collaborative law process.) Collaborative law is currently available in only a few states— California, Minnesota, Ohio, Oregon, and Texas—but it is catching on rapidly across the country.

What are the benefits of collaborative law?

For one thing, it can be cheaper and less anxiety-provoking than using either a mediator or an arbitrator (see below). It's also an amicable way for you and your spouse to settle your differences, and it can pave the way toward a much more cooperative relationship in the future, which is particularly important if there are children involved.

What are the disadvantages of collaborative law?

One of the biggest drawbacks of collaborative law is that if it doesn't work and you end up needing the court to step in and intervene, both your attorney and your husband's attorney must agree to recuse themselves from your case. Basically, you'll each have to hire a new attorney and start all over again. Another risk is that the dynamics of your relationship with your ex—for example, his tendency to bully you—may be replicated in the collaborative-law situation.

What is the difference between this method and using a mediator?

The difference is that a mediator is a neutral third party, whereas in collaborative law, there is no neutral third party present.

MEDIATION

My attorney has suggested that my husband and I explore the possibility of using a mediator. Do you advise this?

I usually recommend that mediation be tried for at least one session. A mediator can help you decide how your property is going to be divided and can also be very helpful in resolving custody arrangements. A mediator is a kind of counselor or referee, and just like a ref, he or she is impartial, with no allegiance to either you or your husband, and works to help you both reach a fair resolution. Please realize that if you are able to reach an agreement with the help of a mediator, it will probably be necessary for you to have your attorneys finalize the agreement and submit it to the court to ensure that it will be binding legally.

Are mediators lawyers?

Many mediators are attorneys, and some are psychologists. The majority of them come from a variety of backgrounds. They can be social workers, marriage counselors, clergymen, or financial experts. They do not need to be licensed, but in some states, they do need to have received specialized training in mediation.

In what circumstances would a mediator not be helpful?

I would not recommend a mediator in cases where custody arrangements or the division of property are unusually complicated, or in cases where emotions are running so high that you can't work together. If you are scared of your spouse for any reason, I would stay away from mediation. I would also keep away from a mediator if you do not feel sure of what your priorities and goals are with respect to negotiation. You should use a mediator only if you and your spouse are able to engage in rational discussion and if you believe you can reach a general agreement about how you want to split things up.

How much do mediators charge?

Depending on what part of the country you live in and the experience and reputation of the mediator in question, he or she will charge anywhere from $60 to $300 an hour. Mediation can work in as few as two hours, or it can last several months, with several sessions scheduled each week.

What happens if mediation works out?

If things work out, then your mediator will usually formalize your agreement in writing. He or she will give each of your attorneys a copy of the agreement to review, and if they give their go-ahead, both of you will sign it. The mediation agreement will be incorporated into your divorce agreement. In some instances, the agreement is signed right after the mediation is concluded, especially if your attorneys have been present during the negotiations.

ARBITRATION

What is the difference between a mediator and an arbitrator? In what situation would it be wise to use an arbitrator?

If you are in a situation where you don't want your divorce to go to trial in a formal courtroom, and you want everything to be legal, but at the same time you are concerned your spouse will manage to get the mediator to see things his way, you might want to seek out an arbitrator. An arbitrator is frequently an attorney, but can also be a retired judge or therapist. In both mediation and arbitration, you avoid going to court, but that's where the similarity ends. Mediation is usually a conciliatory process: You and your spouse agree on who gets what, and in the end, despite the unavoidable pain of divorce, both of you leave satisfied. Most important, the mediator has no power to grant a decision. Arbitration is different because, by definition, the arbitrator can impose a decision on the division of property, just as a judge does. The only differences between an arbitrator and a judge are that you and your spouse select the arbitrator and pay his or her fees rather than using a government-appointed judge, and usually you cannot appeal an arbitrator's decision.

That doesn't sound so bad. What are the downsides of hiring an arbitrator?
Like mediation, arbitration is a private matter. Only the fact of a resolution becomes part of the public record. But mediation is typically much faster than arbitration, in large part because both parties have agreed to conduct themselves in an amicable way. And in effect, you and your spouse are in charge of the outcome. Arbitration, like a court trial, takes that power out of your hands. Remember, the arbitrator is legally allowed to make far-reaching decisions about the allocation of your assets, based on evidence, the facts presented to him and her, and the laws in your particular state. With arbitration, the process is less formal than it would be in court (parties often come to

arbitration sessions without attorneys, though they may consult with them before or after), and usually your attorneys' fees are less, but you each have to pay half the arbitrator's fee. Also, you will have to live with whatever decisions the arbitrator makes. Finally, some people fear that since arbitrators are not really judges, they aren't as qualified to render fair decisions.

Are mediation and arbitration the only two options for us unless my husband and I agree to go to court?
Well, there's also a "marriage" of mediation and arbitration techniques. It's called "med/arb," and it's a little of both. The "med" part assumes that you and your husband will try to work things out in as amicable a way as possible. If this fails, the mediator becomes an "arb," and can make decisions on your and your husband's behalf. To locate a mediator in your state, contact the Academy of Family Mediators at *www.mediators.org*. To locate an arbitrator, you can get in touch with the American Arbitration Association at *www.adr.org*.

The Realities of Divorce

Both my husband and I want to get our divorce over with as quickly and painlessly as possible. What happens after we've met with our attorneys and discussed all our assets?
Once you've met with your attorneys and discussed your assets, it's time to negotiate the settlement. If the marriage has been very short, without children, and there aren't a lot of assets (or debts) to divide, you may be able to divorce through a sum-

mary disposition, which is basically the quickest, most efficient way to file for divorce. In a summary disposition, you and your spouse agree on the basic terms of the dissolution and jointly file simple paperwork with the local court setting forth your plans. Usually, this is done without an attorney (self-representation in legal terms is known as "in pro per"), though in some cases even a summary disposition is done with attorneys or with a joint attorney overseeing the paperwork. In most states, the judge or a research assistant will review the documents and attempt to verify that the agreement is a fair one and that any children involved will be properly cared for. In some states, you may not even have to show up for a court hearing; in other states, a brief hearing may be held, so that the judge can ensure that both sides are getting a fair deal.

What about those cases when a divorce is not friendly?
In these cases, it is not just the best idea for each of you to have an attorney—it is a must. In some cases, even attorneys will not be able to hammer out an agreement and the two of you will have to go before a judge. The attorney's role, as always, is to represent your interests, suggest appropriate settlement items, convey settlement offers, advise you as to what the court is likely to do in your situation, and help with the division of property and debts. The attorney does everything he or she would do in an amicable situation and also fights your battles for you and insulates you from your estranged spouse. Once the terms have been decided—who gets what and when—either by the two of you or with a court order, a marital settlement agreement or stipulated judgment is drafted, which is then used for the final judgment of divorce. If you cannot come to an agreement, you will end up settling your dispute in court.

***It looks like my spouse and I are headed toward court.
What should I keep in mind?***

You should know that the court system, when it comes to divorce, is set up to make sure that the division of property is
handled fairly and to ensure the welfare of any children involved. When you go to court, the outcome is solely in the
hands of the judge. This means that you are putting the fate of
your future, your home, your children, and your pension and
retirement plans in the hands of a total stranger. You should
also know that the court doesn't care whose "fault" the divorce is!

***Are you saying that my husband and I should really try
our best to work out the terms of our divorce instead
of going to court?***

Yes. It won't be easy—in fact, it will be emotional and probably very difficult—but in my opinion, if you and your spouse
can agree on terms between yourselves and reach a clear resolution, you may actually be better off than you would be entrusting your fate and your future to an unknown judge. But if
you simply cannot resolve your differences, you shouldn't be
afraid to put the matter in the hands of a court.

***If my wife and I are already in court, heading toward
trial, is there any way to reach a settlement of some
kind at this point, or is there no turning back?***

There is always room to "turn back" and reach a settlement.
Turning back isn't a failure, it's a solution—and in a lot of
cases, a wise one. Even if you are committed to taking your
spouse to court, an out-of-court settlement may be reached
days or perhaps minutes before the case is to begin. In fact, 90
percent of divorces are settled before trial, no matter how hell-
bent both parties are on having a judge hear their case. How-

ever, I am asking you to be very careful, because this is the time when big mistakes are often made. Imagine this scenario. You are about to go into the courtroom, nervous as can be. Your lawyer, who has been talking in hushed tones to the lawyer representing your ex, approaches you and says your ex is willing to settle the case right now if you give in on a few points. The decision has to be made right away, because once the trial begins it is too late. So you give in on the points and instantly feel a wave of relief . . . but two months down the road, you realize that you may have made a mistake solely to avoid a courtroom confrontation. Do not make decisions that will affect the rest of your life when you feel pressured. If you have gone all the way to trial, do not—unless you know the precise ramifications of everything you may be agreeing to—accept a last-minute settlement.

With our court date just a few weeks away, my estranged husband has offered me a certain amount of money in a one-time payoff. This seems to me more attractive than receiving money from him every month, because I can put him and our marriage behind me. Any advice?

I wouldn't accept his offer. In some instances, a spouse who is required to pay spousal support may instead offer a one-time, lump-sum offer of settlement, which in effect is a "buy-out" of any future obligations, excluding child support. A once-and-for-all settlement is a gamble, because the spouse required to pay is using today's dollars to settle what might be a significantly greater amount tomorrow. If you are considering a settlement, consider all the factors, not just by today's standards but also by tomorrow's. You also need to check out all the tax implications of such an arrangement.

Six months after I filed for divorce, my day in court is finally here. I am extremely nervous. What happens during a trial?

Courtroom trials are fairly predictable and never particularly fluid—that is, they stop and start, and stop again. After opening statements, the court hears the case of the plaintiff (that's you). This is followed by a cross-examination by the attorney for the defendant (your spouse), which is followed by redirect (your attorney's chance to cross-examine the cross-examination). Next the defendant's case is presented, followed by a rebuttal by the plaintiff's attorney, and then, typically, there are closing arguments. Depending on how complex your case is, the judge may issue his or her decision immediately, or choose to deliberate for a while and then issue a written decision.

What happens after the judge issues his or her decision?

Then usually the attorney for the person who prevailed in court drafts a divorce decree. A divorce decree is basically a summary of the judge's decision, which also includes whatever matters you and your spouse decided between yourselves. After the decree is sent to the opposing counsel, it is submitted to the court for its approval.

Can my ex-husband or I appeal the judge's decision?

If you have a legal basis for appeal, of course you can. You cannot mount an appeal simply because you happen not to like his or her decision. Remember, an appeal takes time and money, and the trial court's decision is rarely overturned. For people who have just spent a lot of money on attorneys' fees, the notion of spending even more money—and prolonging the agony of divorce—often doesn't seem very appealing. A much more efficient way to deal with one or more aspects of the judge's decision that rub you the wrong way is to file a petition for modification. This basically leaves the judge's decision in place, but requests that the court modify one or more provisions that you do not like.

Does the divorce decree affect any pretrial court orders?
Yes. Typically, it replaces them.

Assuming that neither of us appeals the judge's decision, now what?
Now a record of your divorce decree is filed at the county courthouse and you are officially divorced. For better or for worse. This is the time to make sure that all your documents—the deed to your house, the title to your car or boat, your will or trust, your insurance policies, and every investment or asset that was previously held jointly—reflect your new status. Please don't let this paperwork slide, for decisiveness will help the healing, the closure, and make you feel stronger for having put your past behind you. With the clutter behind you, you'll be freer to put your energies into starting over again.

LIFE AFTER DIVORCE

For years, my husband and I filed joint tax returns. Now that we're no longer married, do I simply go back to filing singly? If so, at what point do I start doing this?
Any and all income you earn from the date of separation may, if you choose, be filed on a separate tax return. There may be tax ramifications, possibly negative, when you decide to do

this, so make sure you consult an accountant. If you still have any doubt as to what you should do, or if you and your spouse cannot decide how you should file your taxes, file separately. The law allows people who file separately to amend their taxes within a three-year period and to file again jointly, but the law does not let people who file jointly amend their taxes later to file separately.

If you file separately, you and your spouse must decide together how you will divide deductions—the home mortgage interest, charitable deductions that you made together, property taxes, day-care expenses, etc. You will also need to allocate income from joint accounts to one or both spouses for next year's tax returns.

When filing jointly, each of you is liable for what the other puts on your tax return. Be particularly wary if you distrust your spouse when it comes to money. If your spouse overstates deductions or understates income and the IRS catches it, you as well as your spouse will be held responsible for all back taxes and penalties, plus interest. If your now ex-spouse cannot pay these back taxes and penalties, the IRS will come after you. So if money has been a problem between the two of you, you might want to protect yourself and file separately for peace of mind, even if it will cost you more.

My ex-wife is getting in the way of my visitation rights with my children. What should I do?

I will tell you what you should not do, and that is withhold money that the court mandated that you send her for child support. That is not only breaking the law, it could also threaten your children's well-being. If you and your ex-wife aren't really speaking to each other and can't work this out civilly, then you must file a complaint for contempt of court against her. Unless your ex can prove that she has very good reasons for keeping you away from your kids, she will be ordered by the court to do what is legal.

My husband is continually late with his child support payments. Is there anything I can do?
Unfortunately, you are not alone. The legal term for past-due child support is arrearage, and it is a national shame. If I were you, I would hire an attorney to go after your husband, assuming he has some money to chase after. A less expensive method is to contact your state's Child Support Enforcement (CSE) program.

If your spouse is behind in child support payments, you may be able to engage the help of a government official, either someone from the IRS or a child support enforcement advocate, to seize the assets of your errant spouse. Whether to hire your own attorney or rely on the government depends on the type of debt and the laws of your particular state.

What about these private child support collection agencies I keep reading about in the newspaper?
Working with one of these agencies is a possibility, but I would check out their fees very carefully first. Some of them take a huge chunk of any money they recover on behalf of your children.

THE DEATH OF A LOVED ONE

My husband of six years recently died after a short, unexpected illness. I feel utterly wiped out, emotionally. How can I start to put my life in order?
To have someone you love taken from you forever creates a pain so deep that there is little anyone can say or do to help.

Hard as it is to believe in the days, weeks, and months after a death, healing is a function of faith, courage, and time. Having faced the emotional and financial aftermath of death many times with my clients, I have come to believe that we never quite know the meaning of life until we draw close to death. Everything is put into perspective, and in our grief, most of us put thoughts of money at the bottom of our list of priorities— which can be a terrible mistake. The death of a partner forces us not only to deal with a new emotional reality, but also to accept a new financial reality.

I am totally unprepared to deal with financial matters in the midst of all this emotion! Do you have any suggestions?

Allow yourself time to grieve and to heal—but be mindful that the longer you ignore the financial consequences of a spouse's death, the harder it will be to pick up the pieces once you feel ready to take charge of them. Over the years, I have been called upon many times to pick up the financial pieces scattered after a death. Some people who came to me were lucky; when their spouses or life partners died, they had a friend or someone they could trust to help them on their new financial course. But many bereaved souls had sought the advice of a so-called professional when they were most vulnerable and ended up losing everything, or nearly so. By the time they found their way to me, these people had handed over their life insurance proceeds, their portfolios—their futures—to con artists posing as concerned professionals or to commission-hungry sales-people. It is hard enough to find the courage to go on living after you have lost your emotional equilibrium, but it is almost impossible when you have lost your financial stability, too. Difficult as it may seem to you now, in the early stages of your grief, I ask you please to keep your financial realities in mind as you come to terms with the death of your spouse or life partner. The actions you take at this time will have important effects later, when the death and your grief are not so new and raw.

What should I do exactly?

I believe very strongly that in order to assure yourself a smooth passage through this lifetime, you must, out of respect for yourself and your loved ones, plan carefully for your death as early and as thoroughly as you can. Whether there is very little money at stake, or a lot, those who survive your death deserve to grieve without the further burdens of fear and confusion about what will happen to them after you are gone.

My late husband never said anything about money—he said he didn't want to worry me. What should I have done?

For those of you who are in a position to learn about your finances from your loved ones, I beg you not to put this topic off a minute longer. Discuss with your spouse or partner everything you need to know about your estate—including insurance, the children's best interests, the location of all documents, and a list of whom to notify. I urge you to make your preferences clear—whether you wish to be buried or cremated, where you would like your remains to rest, and what kind of service or ceremony you would like to have. A loved one's death is overwhelming, but having some of the details worked out and a sense of purpose in those first painful days will provide you some relief.

When you have just suffered a loss, it's not the time to start learning about money. When you are in a marriage or other close relationship, it is vital—and I cannot stress this enough—that both of you know everything there is to know about your money. Not only how to spend it, but how to invest it and why. Both of you should know where all your important documents are and should know the answer to this question: If one of you were to die tomorrow, would there be enough income for the other person to be financially secure? Please ask this question while your partner is still around to be able to answer it. Little by little, step by step, you can and must learn to handle your money and make decisions that will be right for you in the long run.

My mother, who is 70, lives in Florida and has a burial plot in New York. She recently called and asked me if I thought it was wise for her to prepay her funeral expenses. She has been quoted a package which would send her body back to New York and pay for the chapel, the rabbi, and the cemetery fees, all for under $4,000. What should I tell her?

Well, my first words of advice would be for you to look at some basic numbers: Actuarially speaking, your mother is likely to live another 17 years. If she takes that $4,000 today and invests it in a good no-load mutual fund that averages a 10-percent return, in 17 years that $4,000 will be worth $20,218. If you then adjust for inflation at, say, 3 percent, that $20,218 would be worth $12,232 in today's dollars. So the question is, does your mom really want to spend more than $12,000 to make sure everything is prepaid?

Doesn't her peace of mind make the prepaid funeral worth it?

Yes—but think about it. Not only does she lose the investment potential of her $4,000, buying this package leaves her no room to change her mind about her funeral arrangements!

What if she meets a wonderful man in Florida, marries him, and decides she would like to be buried with him? What if she becomes a Buddhist and decides she would like a different sort of funeral? If you think people don't make those changes at her age, you could be in for a big surprise. So the short answer to your question is, I think prepaid funerals are a waste of money.

My wife just died very suddenly, and my children and I are devastated. It's hard to think about funeral arrangements at this time, but I have no choice. Where should I start?

The shock of losing someone you love can be paralyzing—but you must take care of the business of death, which at the time can seem as complicated as the business of life. Here is a checklist of matters that will require your immediate attention, whether you feel like attending to them or not. If you have a friend or a relative who can assist you, please ask for their help. Even though you may think you are aware and totally capable, you are probably in shock. Temporary numbness may prevent you from collapsing, but it also can impair your ability to make the best and most appropriate decisions.

- The first job that you will be faced with will be making proper arrangements for the burial or cremation of the person you loved. If you are not certain of the deceased's wishes, before you do anything else, please check to see if there is an organ donor card on the back of his or her driver's license. If there is, please contact the nearest hospital so that these wishes can be carried out. Now you must contend with the remains, surely one of the most painful tasks you'll have to perform, but I want you to take care and pay attention, for these first moves can become emotionally and financially costly if you or someone close to you is not vigilant and well informed.

• If the death took place in a hospital, you will be asked the name of the funeral home that you would like to use. The hospital staff will call the funeral home and take care of transporting the remains to the home.

• If the death took place at your home or anywhere other than a hospital, you will have to contact the funeral home or cremation society of your choice, which will then make arrangements to transport the remains.

• If you want the burial or cremation to take place in a state different from the one in which your loved one has died, again, either you or the hospital will place the call to the out-of-state funeral home or cremation society you want to use, and the funeral home will take care of the transportation arrangements for you.

• If you don't know which funeral home you want to use, ask your friends, your clergyman, or an administrator at your local place of worship for a recommendation. Most churches or synagogues have a list of funeral homes for you to call. If you do not have this outlet, and none of your friends can make a recommendation, call your local hospital for assistance.

I've heard horror stories about funeral homes ripping off grieving survivors. When I go in, what should I be aware of?

To make sure that you are not taken advantage of during this vulnerable time, the government many years ago passed a law called the Funeral Rule, which states that a funeral home must provide you with a full disclosure of its practices, services, and fees. This includes the cost of caskets, obituary notices placed in newspapers, and embalming; any payments made on your behalf for flowers, funeral escorts, honorarium to clergy, limousines, copies of the death certificate, memorial cards, and musicians' fees; and any additional service fee that the funeral home may charge. If you wish, you can obtain this list from a number of funeral homes so that you can compare costs. If you are not happy with the available funeral arrangements for any reason, please talk to the funeral director first, and if the problem is still not resolved to your satisfaction, contact your state licensing board.

Unless you or someone else planned for this ahead of time, the funeral home or cremation society will discuss with you whether you need a burial plot, and can assist you in making arrangements to purchase one.

When it comes to planning the service, carefully consider your options. You needn't try to prove your love by choosing the most expensive options available. Dignity, remember, costs not a penny. If you know what kind of service your partner wanted, so much the better. One often hears of people who choose the music they'd like to have played at their funeral services, and the survivors cherish that music forever. If you don't know of any clear preferences of the deceased, your options are many. The service can be held at the funeral home or a place of worship. The burial can be public or private, and you can hold a private burial right away and a memorial service later on.

Again, a lot of choices. But so often, a "nothing but the best" attitude prevails, where "best" translates to most expensive. There is nothing more honorable or more loving in a sendoff you can't afford, so I ask you please to aim for restraint. Public and private good-byes can be dignified, holy, and simple at the same time.

My husband is a veteran of two wars, and I'd like to know beforehand how I can arrange a proper veteran's burial when the time comes.

If your partner or loved one was a veteran, he or she may be eligible to be buried in any of the 115 national cemeteries free of charge. If so, veterans' assistance may provide transportation of the remains to the nearest veterans' cemetery, and a marker or a headstone. In a veteran's burial, a U.S. flag will be used to cover the casket and then will be presented to you. If you choose a veteran's burial, you will have to document the fact that the deceased was a veteran. You will need to have proof of his or her:

Rank
Branch of service
Separation papers (Form 214)
Date of entry into the service and date of departure
Date of birth and date of death
The deceased's Social Security number (as well as your own)
Name and address of the executor or trustee of the estate

Can I choose to have my husband buried in a private cemetery as opposed to a national one and still have a military funeral?

Yes. If you use a private cemetery, you still can apply for a burial allowance, a flag, and a government headstone or marker from the Veterans Administration. If you did not know of such an allowance at the time of burial, you have two years from the date of death to apply for a reimbursement. To apply, just look in your phone book to find the number of the VA office nearest you.

A note of caution: Because obituary notices tell the time and date of most funerals, they make your home a target for burglars. As sad as this may seem, please have someone stay in the house during the service to make sure that you do not come home to yet another loss.

My husband was buried only last month. Now comes the hard part—settling back into my life. Any ideas on where to start?

When you are trying to live through a loss of great magnitude, it is all too easy to lose touch with reality—the reality of life and the reality of money. *Especially* of money, since it seems so irrelevant in those first few days after a death. Nevertheless, death is accompanied by unavoidable costs. After the funeral and during your period of mourning, how are you going to pay for the everyday expenses that will continue to come your way? So often we find that nearly every penny we have is in a retirement account, in a life insurance policy, or locked up in equity in our home, where we can't readily get to it. We are left with very little cash to draw upon. If you haven't done so before, you will now have to try to estimate your monthly expenses and take that figure into consideration before you make any choices—particularly any choices regarding funeral or burial services. For instance, let's say you have $8,000 in a savings account and your monthly expenses total $3,000. If you spend $8,000 on the funeral, you'll be unable to pay your bills.

My husband left me a life insurance policy. Won't this take care of things for the short term?

Even if the deceased had a life insurance policy, the insurance company may not release the funds for many months. This is particularly the case if the cause of death is unclear or if the death appears to have been a suicide. I have a friend whose brother died in a car-racing accident. It just so happened that he had raised his life insurance policy from $50,000 to $250,000 the month before his accident. Because of the timing, the insurance company did not release the insurance proceeds until they had thoroughly investigated the possibility of a suicide. In the intervening months, his widow was left in terrible financial straits.

So I should be very careful before I start spending what I think I have?

Yes. Before you do anything, it is essential that you have a clear picture of what you are going to need to get by for the next few months, and where that money is going to come from. My advice, as always, is to have an understanding of your finances long before you find yourself in a tragic situation.

All my friends are offering to pitch in and help me. Should I take them up on their offers?

Most definitely. That's what friends are for. Following a death, I would suggest you ask whomever you have chosen to help you with the funeral arrangements to collect your mail for the next few weeks. It would also be helpful if he or she could see if there are any bills that need to be paid immediately and keep track of when the rest of the bills will come due. If you are corresponding through the mail with respect to any financial matters related to the estate, please ask your friend to make sure that copies are made of any outgoing mail. It is always important to be able to document everything that you said or that someone said on your behalf during a time of sorrow. Later you may remember these early days only as a blur of pain and confusion.

Do I need to contact an attorney or can I do everything myself?

The way your spouse has set up his or her estate will determine the extent to which you will need an attorney to help you get on with your life. If everything the two of you owned was in joint tenancy with right of survivorship (JTWROS), and you are the sole beneficiary of the life insurance proceeds, IRA, or retirement accounts, everything would automatically pass directly to you upon your spouse's death. Similarly, if everything was held in a revocable living trust (a legal entity that holds your assets while you are alive) for your benefit, then settling the estate will be quite easy. Once the appropriate places are presented with a certified copy of the death certificate and whatever other papers these particular institutions may want to see, everything will simply and automatically switch over to your name.

Unfortunately, my husband had lots of different accounts. He didn't have a living trust or a will. Will settling his estate take longer?

Unfortunately, yes. If your partner had a variety of separate accounts, had only a will, had the house title in his or her name only (even if the intent was that it should pass on to you), then the process will be a longer one. Either way, you should contact an attorney within the first few days after your spouse's death. If you do not have an attorney already, please find one who specializes in probate administration to make sure that everything is in order or to help you organize what must be done.

So I will need an attorney. But is there anything I can do, to save time and money?

Yes, particularly money. There are certain things that you could do by yourself or with the help of a friend. For example, a

friend could call the insurance companies and the bank or brokerage firms to find out what paperwork needs to be done to
report the death. The most important part of your immediate
job will be helping to locate and describe all of your loved one's
assets and liabilities—debts, outstanding loans, everything
your loved one owed to the world.

*Now that my husband has died, I'm hearing many new
words whose meanings I'm not sure of. Could you
translate a few of them for me?*

The legalese of death can sometimes seem like a foreign lan-
guage. Below are brief definitions of some of the terms you will
probably come across:

> Decedent: The person who is deceased.
> Executor/Executrix: The man or woman the decedent
> designated to carry out the terms of the will.
> Co-executors/Co-executrixes: The people (more than
> one) the decedent designated to carry out the terms of
> the will.
> Administrator/Administratrix: The person the court as-
> signs to oversee your estate or your spouse's estate if
> there is no will.
> Personal Representative: In some states, when no execu-
> tor or executrix has been appointed, this is the title of
> the court appointee, whether a man or a woman.
> Trustee: If the estate is held in trust, then this is the per-
> son who is responsible for carrying out the terms of the
> trust.

*What precisely are my duties and responsibilities as
the survivor, both to my late spouse and to myself?*

The duties that a spouse or life partner must carry out vary from those of the executor or executrix. Here is an overview of what you should be attending to immediately:

- Order at least 15 certified copies of the death certificate. You will need these in order to collect insurance proceeds and to change names on bank accounts, deeds, and other assets. Please do this right away. The funeral home usually will be able to get the number of certified death certificates you request. Otherwise, your county has an office of vital statistics at the county courthouse, where death, birth, and marriage certificates are kept and can be obtained upon request for a fee.

- If you do not already have one, please open a bank account in your own name.

- If you do not have a credit card in your own name, you may want to wait to notify the credit card companies where you have cards listed in both of your names. While it is illegal for a company to cancel your credit card because your spouse has died, it is not unheard of for them to lower your credit limit if the limit was based on the deceased's income. (It's always a good idea to have a credit card in your name alone, so that over the years, you will build up credit.)

- Do not pay off any credit card debts that were not yours before you check with your attorney or executor. Some attorneys or advisers might advise you not to pay off the deceased's debts, because it's unlikely that creditors will spend the money to come after the estate to recoup small amounts of debt. I disagree with this advice, because I believe that honoring the debt, if possible, is honoring both the dead and the living. If there isn't enough money in the estate to pay off all debts, the probate court has a "schedule" specifying which debts are given priority and the order in which the debts are to be paid—which is why I want you to check with your attorney before you begin paying the debts.

- Review any insurance coverage that the deceased may have had with banks or credit card companies. You may be surprised to find out that some things slipped through the communications cracks. For instance, offers for life insurance at just a small cost every month often come in the mail via a bank statement or credit card bill. Your spouse may have impulsively signed up for such coverage. This kind of thing happens more often than you might think. You may have more than you know. Call every credit card company and bank that your partner or next of kin had accounts with and ask whether they also have an insurance policy in the name of the deceased.

- Consider whether you will have enough money to live on in the coming months or will need money from the estate before it is settled. Go through six months of your and your late spouse's records and estimate your monthly expenses. If there is not enough money in your existing accounts to cover your projected expenses, the amount you need will be requested from a judge in probate court, where the estate will be settled. The judge will decide on a family allowance while the estate is being settled.

- Contact your local Social Security office—or the national office at (800) 772-1213 or on the Web at *www.ssa.gov*—to see if you qualify for any benefits. You will qualify for benefits if:
You are 60 years of age or older.

You are 50 years of age or older and disabled.

You care for a child who is under age 16 or disabled.

If your surviving parent is 62 years of age or older, and you are your parent's primary means of support, you will qualify through Social Security for survivor's benefits.

In addition, Social Security allots a small amount of money—$225—to surviving spouses or minors if they meet certain requirements. Do not overlook that, for sometimes every little bit can help.

If you and your spouse both were collecting Social Security, you might want to stop collecting yours and collect your late spouse's if that amount is higher. In any case, you have to choose whose you will receive.

Your children will get Social Security if:

They are unmarried and under age 18.

They are under age 19 and still in school full time.

They are disabled, no matter how old they are.

• Please make a note: Do not forget that your own will or trust should be changed now, for most likely you have left everything to the person who has just died. Make sure that you change the beneficiary designation on your IRA, life insurance policies, pension plans, 401(k) plans, and any other investment or retirement plan.

I am both the surviving spouse of my late husband and also one of the executors of his estate. Do I have duties in addition to the ones you just named above?

If you are an executor or executrix as well as the surviving spouse, then the following obligations also pertain. Please also note that an executor/trix is held personally and legally responsible for all of these actions. This is not a job that should be taken lightly or treated as a kind of honorarium. The duties of the executor/trix primarily fall into the following categories:

- Paying all outstanding bills, including taxes to the IRS
- Tallying and securing all assets in the estate until they are ready to be distributed among the rightful heirs
- Supervising the settlement procedures and managing the estate during this process
- Distributing all the assets to the designated beneficiaries at the appropriate time.

The following is a legal checklist for the executor/trix.

- Your first job as executor/trix is to locate the will or trust and all assets, including life insurance policies, retirement, bank, and brokerage accounts, and stocks and bonds. If no will can be found, then call the deceased's attorney, if there is one, to see if he or she has a copy of a will. If nothing else, an attorney may know if one was ever written. If no will can be found, the estate passes by what is known as intestate succession, which means that the assets in the estate will be distributed by a formula determined by law. In this case, there will be a court-appointed administrator.
- Once the will is located, it must be submitted to the probate court, where it must be authenticated. This procedure can be done by the executor/trix, or it can be handed over to the attorney in charge. When the will is authenticated, then the executor/trix is officially appointed by a set of papers known as letters testamentary. These are the official documents that legally empower the executor/trix to take action on behalf of the estate.
- The executor/trix must protect the estate. This means that heirs are not allowed to remove any of the assets

that have been left to them until the probate court has granted final approval for distribution.

- During the probate procedure, the executor/trix must keep careful track of all expenses as well as income (receipts, statements, etc.) that the estate pays out and receives.

- If the surviving spouse has not already obtained certified copies of the death certificate, you should obtain at least 15 copies.

- Notify all the insurance companies of the death, including life, disability, auto, and homeowner's insurance companies. Notify all the banks, brokerage firms, mutual fund companies, retirement plans and plan administrators, and any other institution where the decedent had accounts or deeds, or even accounts that were in both spouses' names. This includes the Veterans Administration if the decedent was a veteran.

- Often individual bank accounts in the decedent's name will be changed first to the name of the executor/trix, even if the executor/trix is not the spouse, so that the executor/trix can access funds if needed. However, if a joint tenancy with right of survivorship is involved, that money and title of the account will go directly to the surviving spouse or partner. For example, Jane and John have a bank account held in JTWROS. If John was to die, Jane would get the account immediately. However, if John had an account in his name alone, and John's brother was executor of John's will, the account would first be transferred to his brother's name as executor while the estate was being settled, even if John left everything to Jane. The account would be transferred to Jane's name upon settlement.

- Before any accounts are closed down, please make sure that the financial needs of the surviving spouse are going to be met. It is best to clear it with the attorney before closing down any existing accounts.
- Make a complete inventory of the safety deposit box. After probate is completed, the executor/trix will distribute the contents according to the will. If the key cannot be located, and the surviving spouse's name is not on the box, you won't be able to open it without a court order, although some states permit access to look for such estate-planning documents as wills and trusts. Most states don't seal the boxes anymore, but the bank can make access difficult. If the box is held in the trust, the trustee will have access. Without the key, you will always end up paying the bank $60 or more to "drill" the box open. (Please don't make those you leave behind go through all this. Leave the key and instructions with your other easy-to-find documents for your kids or whoever is going to be the executor/trix or trustee of your own estate.)

Remember, if the estate is to be distributed through a trust, it does not have to go through probate court, and the trustee named in the trust will carry out the actions designated in the trust.

A crucial note: What lives on after you die? The legacy of your work, your kind and generous acts, and the people you love, who will suffer the emotional toll, and possibly the financial toll, of your passing for a long, long time.

How can you help? The care with which you prepare for your own death is a supreme act of love toward those you will one day leave behind. It can help your survivors a great deal emotionally, for facing chaos following a loss makes the loss itself far more painful and frightening. It can also help your survivors a great deal financially, because with careful estate planning, you may save your loved ones thousands of dollars in probate fees, estate taxes, and attorneys' fees.

Won't you take the actions necessary to protect the people you love, emotionally and financially? Will you please do it right away? Seeing to it that the people you love will always be safe in an expansive action, and once you've done so, you'll be the richer for it, closer to clarity, and all the more ready to receive all that you can, for the rest of your life.

My husband died several months ago, and slowly but surely I'm managing to put my life back together. What should I be keeping in mind during this process?

It may feel like small comfort to you now, but sooner or later every single one of us will be faced with the prospect of starting over. At a time in your life when you believe that everything is going great, something happens—a death, an illness, a breakup, a divorce—that leaves you emotionally and perhaps financially exhausted. And starting over from a place of loss can be even harder than starting out for the first time. When you were just starting out in your adult life, you were equipped with hope, dreams, expectations, and strength. These are stripped from you when you're starting with feelings of loss and emptiness. Will any of us be spared the painful test of starting over, one way or another, one day or another? Unfortunately, I don't think so. This test seems to me utterly universal.

As a financial planner, I do know this much: If you are starting over, you already know that you must replenish your strength in order to go on. It is a treacherous time financially as well as emotionally, and you must be very, very careful with your money. Facing the "whats" and "what-ifs" of starting over requires immense courage. Questions come up. Questions like:

What if I can't make it? I've never really handled money
before.

I've never had to work. What if I can't pay my bills?

My husband left me with just a small settlement, and it's
all I have.

What should I do with the money?

What if the insurance money doesn't last?

What do I do now?

***All these questions seem to come down to one thing: I'm
scared!***

There is nothing wrong with being scared. Even though your
own questions may be different, the common denominator is
fear—fear of not making it, fear of failure, fear of tomorrow—
and these fears come at a time of life when you are at your
most vulnerable. That's the bad news. The good news is that,
even though you might not believe it, I have seen men and
women in this very place, who were ready to give up, instead
rise up and create for themselves a new life they love. A life
they call their own.

***How did these men and women get from a place of loss
and fear to a new life?***

How? By drawing on the faith and courage that reside in each
and every one of us. Remember, after a loss, we rejoin the
world of the living. We don't have a choice! And you must en-
deavor, no matter how great the odds, to start over—to honor
your past, your present, and your future. Bear in mind that
your thoughts, words, and actions during this time have the
power to make your life easier.

***Despite my loss, I feel pretty clear-headed these days.
Am I kidding myself?***

In some ways, probably yes. I can't tell you how many times I have sat across from people who had just suffered losses and were starting over. I would review their situations and say, "Okay, we have to do thus and such, and then we will do this and that and finally this." My clients would agree with me, acting as if they totally understood what I was saying, and I would take the necessary actions based on our conversation. Inevitably, six months to a year later, these same clients would come back and say, "Can you tell me why we did what we did with the money?" It became obvious to me that they had not heard a word I had said during the early stages of their grief. It was as if they had been present in body but not in mind. I would explain the reasons for the actions we took again, and this time, my clients would finally get it.

What would you suggest doing financially following a loss of some kind?
Many of us emerge from a divorce or a death of a loved one with some assets which we must protect, perhaps for the first time in our lives. After seeing the ways in which people tend to jeopardize these assets in their grief, their anger, their exhaustion, or their confusion, I have come up with a rule that has never once failed a client of mine:

Take no action with your money other than keeping it safe and sound for at least six months to a year after a loss.

Why do I need to wait six months to a year? I'm not that much of a basket case, am I?
You have just been through a hard time, with the legalities and expenses of divorce, or the hard tasks you've had to take on after a death. I am simply telling you that you are not equipped now—emotionally or financially—to make the big decisions that have to be made about investing your money yourself or

entrusting it to someone else. If your money is in a secure place, a place that has made you feel safe and comfortable up until now, I want you to leave it there and to wait to take any action with your money until your emotional equilibrium is restored. If you feel your money is not currently safe, make those financial changes that will get your money to a safe place, and then do nothing else for the time being.

How can I make sure that my money is being invested safely during this period?
My advice would be to seek out a financial adviser, one who comes highly recommended by a friend who has money under management with that person. If you have no friend who can recommend someone, what you want for now is a fee-based planner, one who does not sell products of any kind. When you go to see this adviser, you may want to take a friend or relative with you for support. This first thing you should say is, "I am not going to buy anything for at least one year. I just want to make sure that the money I have is safe and sound. I want to put any money that is not safe now into a money market fund or Treasuries, and that is all. No new purchases of any kind are to be made on my behalf."

Can I just go to my late or ex-spouse's financial adviser?
Ask yourself this: How many times did the adviser or broker your spouse was using to manage your joint money talk to you before your world fell apart? What often happens is that a financial adviser builds a relationship with one partner. Understandably, it's more convenient for him or her to have a single contact. A separation or death gives an adviser the opportunity to establish a new rapport with the spouse who previously was merely a name on joint documents. Believe me, this opportu-

nity is not lost on the adviser. Remember, this person is very aware of what is going on not only with your money but also in your personal life. If there is to be a divorce, and therefore a dividing of the assets, the adviser is going to be one of the first to know what you each will be left with. If there is a death, the total picture of your finances is right at his or her disposal. So do not be surprised if you get a cozy call from an adviser with whom you have never really had a relationship to ask you to come in and see him or her to go over what to do with the money in your portfolio.

Should I talk to this financial adviser, or use the six-month plan that you suggested earlier?
You should wait. You're not ready. Just because your late spouse or ex-spouse was using a certain adviser does not mean that the same adviser is right for you. I'm not suggesting that this adviser is necessarily wrong for you, only that this is your life, and everyone in it from this point on must be someone with whom you feel safe and comfortable. Ask yourself the following questions:

- Why was it that you never had a relationship with this particular person to begin with?
- If you did have a relationship with him/her, did you like and trust the relationship?
- Did you feel as if he/she had your best interests and concerns at heart, or just those of your spouse/partner?

Bide your time. These questions will answer themselves in due course.

So you're saying I should be careful with all people who have anything potentially to do with my money?

Absolutely. Bear in mind that it's not only burglars who read the obituaries. Cold callers, hungry brokers, and needy financial types all look to the papers to see if they can somehow expand their business. A sympathetic call when you are feeling vulnerable is a self-interested call—and you're not the "self" in question here. Please say that you are grieving now and ask that solicitors who appear out of the blue call back in a year. They won't.

What about insurance? Is there an optimal way to deal with my insurance company?

Yes. If you are entitled to any life insurance proceeds, regardless of the amount, take the payment in full, even if the insurance company tries to persuade you to take it in installments, or offers to invest it or hold on to it for safekeeping. Most insurance proceeds are tax-free, so you will not incur any penalties by taking them in a lump-sum payment. You may need to deposit some cash into a checking account right away to cover immediate expenses. Then put the rest into a money market account or anywhere you know it will be safe, but also accessible, in case you need funds for your living expenses. Leave the money there until you are more emotionally stable, so that you can intelligently decide what to do with it—again, six months to one year later.

What about making other big changes in my life? Should I put these off, too?

Yes, if you can. Over the next few months, I would like you to try to make as few changes in your life as possible. At the same time, I would also like you to begin asking yourself some essential questions. How do you feel about where you are living? Are you frightened by the amount of money it takes just to live? Are there areas in which you could easily cut back your spending? In time, clarity will set in, and you will know what you must do, however painful, whether it's selling the house, taking a job or a second job, or cutting back on what you can do for your children. In time you will be able to do what you decide you need to do.

People first, then money. Whether you are living with someone, married to someone, getting divorced from someone, or starting your life over following the death of someone you love, the "people" in this first law of money probably refers to you. As I said at the beginning of this book, it is hard enough managing our own money, much less tangling ourselves up in other people's finances. Money is power, and power must be carefully attended to in every relationship. Understanding your own and your partner's money and attitude toward money can only make your relationship and your lives smoother. Practical, sensible plans that treasure your past and anticipate your future are part of that understanding. My advice to you is that it is never too late to take control of your finances, no matter how old you are. Do not be scared if you don't know much today, right now. Take a leap of faith and charge in. Information about money and sound strategies for its care will not only multiply your assets, it will decrease your worries. It is my greatest hope that the information in this book diminishes some of your anxiety and encourages you to turn to the future, not with fear but with hope and courage.

ADDITIONAL RESOURCES

BOOKS

The following books are indispensable, whether you are living together, separating, or getting a divorce:

Divorce & Money: How to Make the Best Financial Decisions During Divorce by attorneys Violet Woodhouse, CFP, and Victoria F. Collins, Ph.D., CFP, with M. C. Blakeman. Common-sense strategies for dividing debts, setting alimony, and much more.

The Living Together Kit by attorneys Ralph Warner, Toni Ihara, and Frederick Hertz. Everything unmarried couples need to define and protect their relationship is covered in this superb resource.

Legal Affairs: Essential Advice for Same-Sex Couples, by Frederick Hertz.

A Legal Guide for Lesbian and Gay Couples by attorneys Hayden Curry, Denis Clifford, Robin Leonard, and Frederick Hertz. This excellent volume tells you all you need to make a living-together agreement, handle property, and much more.

Nolo's Pocket Guide to Family Law by attorneys Robin Leonard and Stephen Elias will answer any question you might have regarding adoption, divorce, marriage, custody, and mediation.

ADDITIONAL RESOURCES

INTERNET

www.law.cornell.edu/lii.table.html offers a huge database and search engine, as well as the complete text of various state court decisions.

www.nolopress.com, the Nolo Press website will answer questions about living together, separation, divorce, and child custody, as well as on many other topics.

www.yahoo.com/law/ offers links to many state laws.

FINDING PROFESSIONAL ADVICE

Lawyers

The best resource for evaluating lawyers in your region is the Martindale-Hubbell Directory, which is usually available at your local library. Or you can access the Martindale-Hubbell website at *www.martindale.com,* or their related site at *www.lawyers.com.*

You can reach the American Academy of Matrimonial Lawyers at 150 North Michigan Avenue, Suite 2040, Chicago, IL 60601. Their phone number is (312) 263-6477, and their fax number is (312) 263-7682. You can also access their website at *www.aaml.org.*

Mediation and Arbitration

One very good resource is The Center for Dispute Settlement, 1666 Connecticut Avenue, NW, Suite 500, Washington, D.C. 20009. Their phone number is (202) 265-9572, and their fax number is (202) 328-9162.

The Academy of Family Mediators is located at 5 Militia Drive, Lexington, MA 02173. Their phone number is (781) 674-2663, and their fax number is (781) 674-2960. Or you can access their website at *www.lgc.apc.org/afm,* or *www.mediators.org.*

Appraisers

American Society of Appraisers (business appraisers)
555 Herndon Parkway, Suite 125
Herndon, VA 20170
Telephone: (800) 272-8258
Fax: (703) 742-8471
www.appraisers.org

Appraisal Institute
875 North Michigan Avenue, Suite 2400
Chicago, IL 60611
Telephone: (312) 335-4100
Fax: (312) 335-4474
www.appraisalinstitute.com

The Kelley Blue Book (cars and used cars) can be accessed on the
World Wide Web at *www.kbb.com.*

CHILD SUPPORT

The National Child Support Enforcement Association
Hall of the States
444 North Capitol Street, NW, Suite 414
Washington, D.C. 20001-1512
Telephone: (202) 624-8180
Fax: (202) 624-8828
www.ncsea.org

Administration for Children and Families
U.S. Department of Health and Human Services
Child Support Enforcement
370 L'Enfant Promenade, SW
Washington, D.C. 20447
Telephone: (202) 401-9383
Fax: (202) 401-5559
www.acf.dhhs.gov/programs/cse

ADDITIONAL RESOURCES

TAX QUESTIONS AND ASSISTANCE

The Internal Revenue Service
(800) 829-1040
www.irs.ustreas.gov

SOCIAL SECURITY

Social Security Administration
(800) 772-1213
www.ssa.gov

INDEX

ABOUT THE AUTHOR

Suze Orman is the author of the #1 *New York Times* bestsellers *The 9 Steps to Financial Freedom* and *The Courage to Be Rich* and the national bestseller *You've Earned It, Don't Lose It.* A Certified Financial Planner®, she directed the Suze Orman Financial Group from 1987 to 1997, served as Vice-President of Investments for Prudential-Bache Securities from 1983 to 1987, and from 1980 to 1983 was an account executive at Merrill Lynch. She has hosted two PBS specials, one based on *The 9 Steps to Financial Freedom* and the other on *The Courage to Be Rich,* and is currently a financial contributor to NBC News' *Today.* She lectures widely throughout the United States and has appeared on *Dateline,* CNN, and CNBC, and has made numerous appearances on *The Oprah Winfrey Show.*

Certified Financial Planner® is a federally registered mark owned by the Certified Financial Planner Board of Standards, Inc.